D0993233

11.95

# *Padre Pio's Words of Hope*

*"Be quite at peace as regards the existence of divine love in your heart. Cast aside all that futile anxiety and have no fear."*

## Edited by Eileen Dunn Bertanzetti

Our Sunday Visitor Publishing Division
Our Sunday Visitor, Inc.
Huntington, Indiana 46750

Scripture citations in this work are taken from the *New Revised Standard Version* of the Bible, copyright © 1989 by the Division of Christian Education of the National Council of the Churches of Christ in the United States of America. Published by Thomas Nelson, Inc. Used with permission. Padre Pio's quotes are taken from *Padre Pio of Pietrelcina's Letters*, Volumes I, II, and III, and — except for some minor editing in order to clarify, condense, and create a more inclusive text — are reproduced practically verbatim. Published by San Giovanni Rotondo; used with permission. The illustrations included in the text are by the author, Eileen Dunn Bertanzetti.

ISBN: 0-87973-694-1
LCCCN: 99-70511

Cover design by Monica Watts
694

*For my husband, Greg, through whom God loves and guides me*

# Acknowledgments

I would like to acknowledge the following: Our Sunday Visitor' acquisitions editor Jackie Lindsey and project editor Lisa Grote; my parents Norm and Marie Dunn; my children, Doug, Jill, Lori, Dave, Pete, and Ellen; my mentor Teri Martini; our pastor Monsignor D. Boggs; my friends Father J. Crookston, Father T. Stein, Sister Patricia Edward, Donna, Claude, Dorothy Gaudiose, Barbara, Joanie, Veda, Kristi, Andrea, Carolyn, Sherry, Sally, Carol, Mary Lou, Elizabeth, Olive, and Carmen; my prayer partners the Sinsinawa Dominicans; the Ross Library staff; the Lock Haven University Stevenson Library staff; Father Alessio Parente, O.F.M. Cap., of San Giovanni Rotondo, Italy, for giving me permission to quote Padre Pio's letters; Our Blessed Mother; Padre Pio; my holy guardian angel; and, of course, Christ Our Lord.

# *Table of Contents*

Introduction / 9

Meditations 1-10 / 15

Abandon Into the Divine Arms ✦ Anchor ✦ Anxiety ✦ Battle ✦ Be Yourself ✦ Bread of Life ✦ Bridegroom ✦ Burdens ✦ Calm ✦ God's Care for You

Meditations 11-20 / 26

Charity/Love ✦ Cheerful ✦ Be Like Children ✦ Christian ✦ Christmas All Year ✦ Comfort ✦ Comparison ✦ Condemnation of Self ✦ Confidence in God ✦ Consolation

Meditations 21-30 / 37

Contemplation ✦ Courage ✦ Cross ✦ Dangers ✦ Death ✦ Little Defects ✦ Delight ✦ Desires ✦ Desolation ✦ Devotion Through Humble and Suffering Prayer

Meditations 31-40 / 48

Distractions ✦ Divine Artist ✦ Domestic Life ✦ Dryness of Spirit ✦ Encouragement ✦ Enemy ✦ Eternal Life ✦ Eucharist ✦ Failings ✦ Faith

Meditations 41-50 / 59

Family: Your Boat ✦ Father God ✦ Fear ✦ Food of the Angels ✦ Footsteps of God ✦ Forgive With Love ✦ Freedom in God's Word, God's Will ✦ Friend in the Dark ✦ Future/Eternity ✦ Gifts of God

## Meditations 51-60 / 70

God's Spirit ✦ Gratitude ✦ Guardian Angels ✦ Jesus Our Guide ✦ Handmaid of the Lord ✦ Happiness ✦ Health of Body and Soul ✦ Christ's Heart ✦ Your Heart ✦ Heaven, the Right Port

## Meditations 61-70 / 81

Help Divine ✦ Holy Communion ✦ Holy Spirit ✦ Holy Trinity ✦ Hope ✦ Humility ✦ Hurry at Christ's Every Invitation ✦ Impatience ✦ Imperfections ✦ Like a Child in a Mother's Arms

## Meditations 71-80 / 92

In a World Lost By God ✦ Infant Jesus ✦ Intention to Please God ✦ Intercession ✦ Jesus, Most Compassionate and Tender ✦ Jesus' Sufferings and Yours ✦ Joyfulness ✦ Justification ✦ Kiss of the Divine Mouth ✦ Knock

## Meditations 81-90 / 103

Lest You Dash Your Foot ✦ Life ✦ Little Things ✦ Lord Jesus, Lover of Your Soul ✦ Love of God ✦ Love of Neighbor ✦ Mary Magdalene and You ✦ Mary Most Holy ✦ Maxim of Padre Pio ✦ Meditation

## Meditations 91-100 / 114

Mercy ✦ Misery ✦ My Guardian Dear ✦ Our Blessed Mother Mary ✦ Paradise ✦ Pardoned All ✦ Passion of Jesus ✦ Paths ✦ Patience ✦ Peace

## Meditations 101-110 / 125

Perfection ✦ Power of Jesus' Name ✦ Prayer ✦ Precipice ✦ Presence of God ✦ Trusting in Self/Presumption ✦

Problems ✦ Spiritual Reading ✦ Reflect, Consider ✦ Rejected, Abandoned by God

## Meditations 111-120 / 136

Resigned to God's Will ✦ Resist ✦ Round About You ✦ Sacred Heart of Jesus ✦ Sacred Scripture ✦ Saints ✦ Salvation ✦ Sanctify ✦ Scruples, Sadness, Fear ✦ Seasons of the Soul

## Meditations 121-130 / 147

Seniors, Juniors, Any-Agers ✦ Separated From God? ✦ Servants of the Lord ✦ Silence ✦ Simplicity ✦ Sin ✦ Solitude ✦ Soul ✦ Spouse of Your Soul ✦ Stand Firm on the Word and Law of God

## Meditations 131-140 / 158

Storm ✦ Your Strength ✦ Suffering ✦ Supreme Good ✦ Sweetness ✦ Temple of God ✦ Temptation's Tests ✦ Thanks and Praise ✦ This Kindhearted Angel ✦ Tomorrow

## Meditations 141-150 / 169

Tranquillity, Stillness, Peace ✦ Troubles, Trials, and Tribulations ✦ Trust in God ✦ Unseen ✦ Virtue, Piety ✦ Deep Waters ✦ Weaknesses ✦ When God Hides ✦ Bloom Where You're Planted ✦ Will of God

## Bibliography / 179

## Notes / 180

Padre Pio of Pietrelcina said, "May Jesus keep his gaze turned upon you and enable you to belong to that great multitude — seen by the beloved disciple — which no person could number" (*Letters, Volume I* and Revelation 7:9).

# Introduction

During the eighty-one years of his life, Padre Pio — proclaimed "venerable" by Pope John Paul II on December 18, 1997 — had plenty of reasons to fear, worry, and doubt.

For fifty years, as a monastic priest in San Giovanni Rotondo, Italy, Pio bore the stigmata, the five wounds of Christ crucified. For fifty years those wounds bled, causing Pio's hands to swell, his side to throb, and his feet to ache. Throughout his life, he also endured frequent tests which doctors and scientists performed on his five wounds to see if they had natural or supernatural origin. Every conclusion: Pio's stigmata were not of natural origin.

## Stigmata

Through spiritual as well as bodily fevers, Padre Pio continued to suffer. During every moment of every trial, he trusted in Jesus and found joy in him: On September 20, 1918, while praying alone in the San Giovanni chapel, Pio trembled as an angelic creature materialized in front of him. Blood dripped from the creature's hands, feet, and side. Terror snaked through Pio at the sight, then he cried out as spears of light — radiating from the creature — pierced Pio's own hands, feet, and side. The young priest slumped to the floor. As blood dripped from his five fresh wounds, he thought he would surely die.

But he lived, and in March of 1919, Pio wrote to a friend who had asked about that moment of stigmatization, ". . . since September 18 of last year, after the appearances of that heavenly personage, I found my hands and feet pierced and an open wound close to the heart. I don't want you to begin to hold me, a wretch, in high regard as a result of this revelation. Admire the marvels of the Lord and nothing else."[1]

Even though he had received the gift of Christ's stigmata, it only made Pio feel more undeserving of God's love.

But still he trusted and rejoiced.

## Take Heart

"Live tranquilly and don't be bewildered in the dark night through which your spirit is passing," said Padre Pio. "Be patient and resigned while awaiting the return of your divine Sun who will soon come to brighten the forest of your spirit."[2]

Why did Pio have such undying confidence in Christ? Through his own experiences with pain, poverty, frail health, and other trials, Pio learned to "take heart; it is Jesus who permits your soul to be in a state of aridity, in darkness. . . . The Lord wants to lead you amidst the thorns because he wants you to be similar to him."[3]

## Exile

On June 9, 1931, Pio's superiors suspended him from all priestly duties, except for saying Mass in private. Even though word of his stigmata and other spiritual gifts had already spread around the globe, the Church — in her wisdom — needed time to investigate these phenomena before allowing the faithful to continue to flock to the San Giovanni monastery where Pio lived.

Were the miracles people claimed had come to them through Padre Pio really from God? Or did those miracles arise from twisted minds and natural causes? Two long years later, when the Church finally allowed Pio to resume his priestly duties, his followers celebrated. God had seen and heard their tears and prayers during Pio's exile.

## Some of His Other Gifts

For fifty years, Padre Pio bore the gift of the stigmata. Wasn't that enough for one person? Apparently not. In order to help people, God also blessed Pio with the gift of bilocation — the ability to be in two places at one time.

Pio had the gift of perfume. Many times when he wanted people to know he was praying for them and that God would meet their needs, the people would smell violets, lilies, and roses. In Confession, Padre Pio had the ability to read a person's soul. If the person concealed sins from him, Pio would reveal them to that person.

God also granted Pio the gift of conversion. Countless people returned to Jesus and the Church through Padre Pio's intercession.

By Christ's power, Pio healed the sick in body, mind, and soul. Padre Pio also prophesied. During World War II, he told the people of San Giovanni Rotondo that no bombs would hit that city. With a foreign-occupied air base only fifteen miles away, the people refused to believe their Padre. But when the war ended and no bombs had struck their town, they believed.

Though Padre Pio received more than his share of spiritual gifts, he never sought them, never felt worthy of them. He never put the gifts before the giver. About supernatural gifts, Pio wrote, ". . . you must by no means desire such extraordinary things, knowing that it is not these things that render the soul more perfect, but rather, holy Christian virtue."[4]

## Pilgrims From Around the World

In spite of — and because of — all his spiritual gifts, Padre Pio suffered in many ways. The gifts attracted pilgrims from all over the world. People traveled to the rocky, barren land on which San Giovanni perched. They wanted to see, touch, hear, and even smell this now-famous priest. Women came with scissors and tried to snip off pieces of his brown garments to take home as souvenirs. More than once he had to scold people who crowded around him so tightly he thought he might suffocate.

Because Pio hated to be the center of attention, his popularity caused him inner pain. But despite all his afflictions of body and soul, he continued to trust Christ and to find great joy in God. ". . . From long experience," Pio said, "I know there was absolutely no way Jesus would either remove or alleviate all those gifts he has given me up to now. So I will stretch myself out on this cross, also in a placid manner, and with a serene soul. . . ."[5]

## Heavenly Homeland

By 1968, the year of Pio's death, millions of people revered him, but others still mocked him. Some newspapers claimed that Pio "faked" the stigmata and other spiritual gifts. Some of the faithful at his Masses glanced at their watches and tapped their toes because they wanted him to hurry through the prayers. But Pio *lived* the Mass and often fell into ecstasy, in love with God present in the Eucharist.

No matter what troubles assailed him, Pio refused to let his "heart be troubled."[6] He trusted Jesus. "Pay no attention to the path of trial," Pio wrote, "but I invite you to keep your eyes constantly fixed on he who guides you to the heavenly homeland. Why should the soul be despondent? . . . Believe me, Jesus is with you, so what do you fear?"[7]

No matter what trials you face, remember what Padre Pio said, "Call to mind the words the divine Master said to the Apostles, and which he says to you today, 'Do not let your hearts be troubled.' "[8]

# Padre Pio

1887, May 25 — born in Pietrelcina, Italy

1903, January — entered Capuchin Novitiate in Morcone

1910, August — ordained in Cathedral of Benevento

1918, September — received stigmata

1947, May — inaugurated Home for the Relief of Suffering

1968, September 22 — celebrated last Mass

1968, September 23 — died

1997, December 18 — proclaimed "venerable"

1999, May 2 — beatified

Through letters, Padre Pio guided and encouraged the faithful. "As regards your own soul, have no fear. Jesus is living in you" (*Letters, Volume I*).

# *Abandon Into the Divine Arms*

Matthew 16:24-25: "Then Jesus told his disciples, 'If any want to become my followers, let them deny themselves and take up their cross and follow me. For those who want to save their life will lose it, and those who lose their life for my sake will find it.' "[1]

*But I fear letting go and following God.*

Padre Pio's assurance: "Oh, how well-protected is that soul whom God has gathered beneath his wings. Yes, she can well sit down and rest in utter peace in this shade, for he who fills her with many graces will not allow her to fall. Jesus wants her wholly for himself. Let this precious jewel renew her faith, let her cast herself with sublime abandonment into the arms of God, and he will fulfill the plans he has for her."[2]

"It is the Lord who works within you," said Padre Pio, "and you must do nothing except leave the door of your heart wide open so that he might work as he pleases."[3]

"Let the Holy Spirit accomplish what he wants in you. Abandon yourself to his transports and do not fear. He is so discreet, wise, and sweet that he cannot but do good."[4]

*Enter, Lord, and do as you will. Amen.*

# Anchor

Hebrews 6:18-19: ". . . seize the hope set before us. We have this hope, a sure and steadfast anchor of the soul. . . ."[1]

*But how can I hold on while problems try to strangle me?*

Padre Pio's assurance: "I consider what writers say about the kingfisher, little birds who build their nests on the beach near the sea. They build in a circular form and so tightly compressed that the seawater cannot penetrate the nest. Above is an opening from which they receive air. Here, these graceful little birds place their young ones, so that when the sea comes upon them by surprise, they can swim with confidence and float on the waves without being filled with water or submerging. And the air they breathe through that opening serves as a counter-balance so that those little balls of fluff are not overturned."[2]

"But, what amazes me most of all is that the anchor is cast above them and not below, in order to strengthen them against the waves."[3] "I want your heart to be like this, well-compacted and closed on all sides so that . . . it will not be penetrated [by worries and evil]. Leave but one opening to your heart, that is, one toward heaven. . . ."[4]

*Lord, anchor me to yourself so that trials cannot defeat me. Amen.*

# *Anxiety*

Matthew 6:25, 32, 34: "Therefore I tell you, do not worry about your life, what you will eat or what you will drink, or about your body, what you will wear. . . . Your heavenly Father knows that you need all these things.

". . . So do not worry. . . ."[1]

*But my needs burden my mind. How can I not worry?*

Padre Pio's assurance: "Do not anticipate the problems of this life with apprehension, but, rather, with a perfect hope that God, to whom you belong, will free you from them accordingly. He has defended you up to now. Simply hold on tightly to the hand of his divine providence, and he will help you in all events, and when you are unable to walk, he will lead you; don't worry. . . . Don't think about tomorrow's events because the same heavenly Father who takes care of you today will do the same tomorrow and forever.

"Live tranquilly. Remove from your imagination that which upsets you, and often say to the Lord, 'Oh, God, you are my God, and I will trust in you. You will assist me and be my refuge, and I will fear nothing.' . . ."[2]

*Forgive me for worrying, Lord. I place my trust in you. Amen.*

# *Battle*

Ephesians 6:14-17: "Stand therefore, and fasten the belt of truth around your waist, and put on the breastplate of righteousness. As shoes for your feet put on whatever will make you ready to proclaim the gospel of peace. With all of these, take the shield of faith, with which you will be able to quench all the flaming arrows of the evil one. Take the helmet of salvation, and the sword of the Spirit, which is the word of God."[1]

*But in the heat of battle, the struggle threatens to overwhelm me.*

Padre Pio's assurance: "Let us face the present trials to which divine providence subjects us, but let us not lose heart or become discouraged. Let us fight valiantly, and we will obtain the prize of strong souls. Remember the words the divine Master spoke one day to the Apostles and which he says to you today, 'Do not let your hearts be troubled.'[2] Yes, let not your heart be troubled in the hour of trial because Jesus promised his real assistance to those who follow him.

"Therefore, in the hour of battle, let us remember Jesus who is with us, and who suffers with us and for us. Let us remember Jesus fighting for us and with us. Let us ask him, and we will always obtain relief."[3]

*Lord, help me to remember at all times that you rejoice and suffer with me, in me, and for me, and that you have already won the battle. Amen.*

# *Be Yourself*

Romans 12:4-6: "For as in one body we have many members, and not all the members have the same function, so we, who are many, are one body in Christ, and individually we are members one of another. We have gifts that differ according to the grace given to us. . . ."[1]

*But sometimes it seems as if I have no gifts at all, no ability to help anyone or to do anything of importance.*

Padre Pio's assurance: "Do not scatter the seed in the gardens of others, but cultivate your own. Don't desire to be anything but what you are. Concentrate on perfecting yourself and on carrying the crosses, either small or large, that you will encounter on your journey to heaven. And believe me that this is the most important advice, but also the least understood in spiritual behavior: Each one loves according to his own tastes. Few, however, live according to their duty and the will of the Lord. From this there arises that tearful state whereby many start out on the path to perfection, but few arrive at the summit of the same perfection."[2]

*Help me, Lord, to appreciate what you have given me: Gifts — no matter how small or few. Family and friends — whether near or far. Material goods — no matter how much or how little. But most of all, please help me to cherish your constant presence and love. Amen.*

# Bread of Life

Luke 6:18-19: "They had come to hear him [Jesus] and to be healed of their diseases; and those who were troubled with unclean spirits were cured. And all in the crowd were trying to touch him, for power came out from him and healed all of them."[1]

*But does God still heal bodies, minds, and spirits?*

Padre Pio's assurance: "You must never fail to approach the holy Banquet of the divine Lamb, as nothing will better gather your spirit than its King. . . . There is no remedy more powerful than this."[2]

"Ah, Father, I cannot ask you to remove Jesus from among us . . . how could I who am so weak and half-hearted live without this Eucharistic food? How could I fulfill that petition made by your Son in our name, 'Your will be done, on earth as it is in heaven,'[3] if I did not receive strength from this immaculate flesh?"[4]

"We must always have courage, and if some spiritual languor comes upon us, let us run to the feet of Jesus in the Blessed Sacrament, and let us place ourselves in the midst of the heavenly perfumes, and we will undoubtedly regain our strength."[5]

*Enable me, Lord, to receive your healing touch in the Eucharist. Amen.*

# Bridegroom

John 3:29: "The friend of the bridegroom, who stands and hears him, rejoices greatly at the bridegroom's voice. For this reason my joy has been fulfilled."[1]

*But so often my desires scream at me while God, our bridegroom, whispers. How can I learn to hear his voice?*

Padre Pio's assurance: "Jesus loves you; he wants you to belong totally to him. . . . Don't look anywhere else, and don't let your soul dwell on anyone except him. Keep your will thus simply united to him so that there is nothing between you and God.

"Don't think of what you are unable to do, but rather, think of what you can do, and do it well, for the love of the bridegroom. . . . You have already placed everything in God. Clothe yourself in our Lord Jesus Christ crucified; love him in his sufferings, say many short ejaculatory prayers while thinking of this."[2]

"Your soul is in the arms of your divine spouse, like a baby in its mother's arms. You may sleep in peace, therefore, for this heavenly spouse will guide you in the way which is to your greatest advantage."[3]

*Lord, forgive me for listening to myself rather than to you. Take over my life and help me to always hear and follow your voice. Amen.*

# *Burdens*

Matthew 11:28-30: "Come to me, all you that are weary and are carrying heavy burdens, and I will give you rest. Take my yoke upon you, and learn from me; for I am gentle and humble in heart, and you will find rest for your souls. For my yoke is easy, and my burden is light."[1]

*But often I try to shoulder self-imposed burdens alone, and I fail.*

Padre Pio's assurance: "May Jesus enable you to appreciate more and more, along with all the souls who love him with a sincere and pure heart, his most loving invitation: 'My yoke is easy, and my burden is light.'[2] May this tender invitation of the divine Master console you in this trial. . . ."[3]

"We must become familiar with the sufferings Jesus will be pleased to send us as if we were to live with them always. Thus, when you least expect to be set free, Jesus, who cannot bear to see you suffer for a long time, will take care of it. He will come to relieve and console you, by instilling new courage in your soul."[4]

". . . When he bestows a cross on one of his chosen ones, he strengthens that soul to such an extent that by bearing the weight of this cross the soul is relieved of it."[5]

*Lord, help me to always go to you with my burdens, knowing that you will either take them away or give me the strength to bear them. Amen.*

# *Calm*

Psalm 107:28-29: "Then they cried to the Lord in their trouble, / and he brought them out from their distress; / he made the storm be still, / and the waves of the sea were hushed."[1]

*But how can I allow God to calm me when people and things storm into my life?*

Padre Pio's assurance: "We should turn our thoughts to heaven, our true homeland, of which our earthly country is but a dim image, and make every effort, with the divine assistance, to preserve at all times, amidst happy or sad events, the cheerful calm that becomes the true followers of the fair Nazarene."[2]

"We should be on the alert for every slightest sign of agitation, and as soon as we realize we have fallen into dejection, we must turn to God with filial confidence and abandon ourselves completely to him."[3]

"If we keep our souls calm and peaceful in every difficult situation, we will gain much ground in the ways of God. On the other hand, if we lose this peace, everything we do with a view to eternal life will yield little or no fruit."[4]

*Lord, help me to always turn to you and allow you to restore calm within me, even when storms rage on the outside. Amen.*

# God's Care for You

1 Peter 5:7: "Cast all your anxiety on him, because he cares for you."[1]

*But when I take a close look at myself, I see only sin and weakness, and I can't believe that God would want to help me.*

Padre Pio's assurance: "Think no more of your past life, except in order to admire the heavenly Father's goodness which . . . did not want to reject you, but rather, with great care, wished to overcome your hardness and, winning you over with his grace, wanted and wants to demonstrate his power over you."[2]

"Place all your cares in God alone because God cares greatly for you."[3]

"Let us consider Jesus' love for us and his concern for our well-being, and then let us be at peace. Let us not doubt that he will invariably assist us with fatherly care against all our enemies. If it were left to ourselves to remain on our feet, we should never be able to do it. At the first breath of air we should fall down and certainly have no hope of rising again."[4]

". . . How many times does he not stretch out his hand to us to arrest our headlong dash towards the precipice? How many times, when we had abandoned him, has he not readmitted us to his loving embrace?"[5]

*Lord, help me to remember that you love me more than I can imagine, and that, despite my sin and weakness, you always want to help me. Amen.*

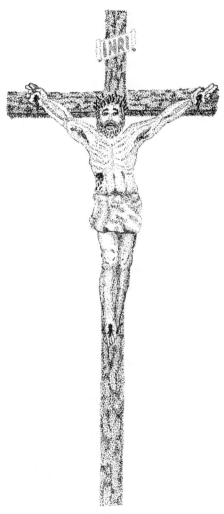

On September 20, 1918, Padre Pio received the stigmata, the five bleeding wounds of Christ, while praying before the crucifix in the old church of the monastery at San Giovanni Rotondo. "I love the Cross because I see it always on Jesus' shoulders. My entire life, my whole heart is consecrated to him and to his sufferings" (*Letters, Volume I*).

# Charity/Love

Colossians 3:14: "Above all, clothe yourselves with love, which binds everything together in perfect harmony."[1]

*But how am I supposed to love when all I want to do is strike out at the world and everyone in it for all the injustice, turmoil, and pain?*

Padre Pio's assurance: "Grow always in Christian love and never tire of advancing in this which is the queen of all the virtues. Consider that you can never grow too much in this most beautiful virtue. Love it very much. Let it be more than the apple of your eye, for it is truly most dear to our divine Master. . . . Oh, yes, let us greatly esteem this precept of the divine Master, and all difficulties will be overcome.

"The virtue of love is exceedingly beautiful, and to enkindle it in our hearts the Son of God was pleased to come down himself from the bosom of the eternal Father, to become like us in order to teach us and make it easy for us, with the means he left us, to acquire this most eminent virtue.

"Let us ask Jesus insistently to give us this virtue, and let us make greater and greater efforts to grow in it. Let us ask this, I repeat, at all times and more than ever. . . ."[2]

*Lord, give me the grace to continually grow in love. Show me how to let go of frustration, anger, and all that keeps me from love. Amen.*

# *Cheerful*

Proverbs 15:13: "A glad heart makes a cheerful countenance. . . ."[1]

*But how can I look and act cheerful when darkness shrouds my heart?*

Padre Pio's assurance: "You must be strong and cheerful in spirit, for the Lord is in the depths of your heart."[2]

"Keep cheerful and don't be discouraged."[3]

"Never permit your soul to become sad — to live with a sad scrupulous spirit — because Jesus is the spirit of sweetness. . . ."[4]

"Let us show ourselves to be worthy children of such a great Father. Jesus also invites us to climb to Calvary with him, so let us not refuse. Ascending the painful mount with Jesus will be a joy for us. In the course of life, mortifications will not be lacking for us either. Let us love them; let us embrace them with a cheerful soul, and let us always bless the good God in everything."[5]

"I thank the Lord that despite the fact that . . . I suffer moments of real anguish, I am invariably cheerful. . . .

"Meanwhile, I cast myself trustfully into the arms of Jesus, then let whatever he has decreed take place, and he must certainly come to my aid."[6]

*Jesus, take me in your arms and do as you will. Dwell in me, and let your peace and cheerfulness permeate my heart. Amen.*

# Be Like Children

Luke 18:16-17: "But Jesus called for them and said, 'Let the little children come to me, and do not stop them; for it is to such as these that the kingdom of God belongs. Truly I tell you, whoever does not receive the kingdom of God as a little child will never enter it.' "[1]

*But every day I bear the trials and responsibilities of an adult; how can I receive God and his kingdom as a little child would do?*

Padre Pio's assurances: "Be like children. They almost never think about their future, as they have somebody to think of it for them. They are only strong enough when they are with their parent. Therefore, you do the same, and you will be in peace."[2]

"Place the outcome of your desires in the hands of divine providence, and abandon yourself in God's arms like a child, who, in order to grow, eats what his parent gives him every day, hoping his parent will not leave him without food in proportion to his appetite and necessities."[3]

"To be afraid of being lost while you are in the arms of divine goodness is stranger than fear on the part of a child in its mother's arms. Get rid of all doubt and anxiety. . . ."[4]

*Lord, I can't go back to my childhood, but I can place myself in your ever-loving parental embrace. I do so now. Amen.*

# *Christian*

Colossians 3:16-17: "Let the word of Christ dwell in you richly; teach and admonish one another in all wisdom; and with gratitude in your hearts sing psalms, hymns, and spiritual songs to God. An whatever you do . . . do everything in the name of the Lord Jesus, giving thanks to God the Father through him."[1]

*But too often I have no wisdom, no song, no gratitude to offer.*

Padre Pio's assurance: "If the Christian is full of God's law which warns and teaches him to despise the world and its allurements, wealth and honors, and all that prevents him from loving God, he will never fail, no matter what adversities may befall him; he will endure everything steadfastly and perseveringly; he will readily forgive offenses and give thanks to God for all things.

"The Apostle [Paul] wants God's law and Jesus' doctrine to be and to dwell abundantly in us. Now all this cannot come about unless we apply ourselves to reading holy scripture and books dealing with divine things, listening to God's word as expounded by holy preachers . . . diligent application to meditation on God's law, which makes the Christian exult with joy and chant sweet psalms and hymns to God."[2]

*By the power of your Holy Spirit, teach me to fill myself with Christ's word, wisdom, and law, so that gratitude always flows from me to you. Amen.*

# Christmas All Year

Matthew 2:10-11:"When they saw that the star had stopped, they were overwhelmed with joy. On entering the house, they saw the child with Mary his mother; and they knelt down and paid him homage. Then, opening their treasure chests, they offered him gifts of gold, frankincense, and myrrh."[1]

*I'd like to stay with Mary beside her Son's crib, but, except during each Christmas season, I don't experience the Christ child's presence.*

Padre Pio's assurance: "Our Lord loves you, and he loves you tenderly. And if he doesn't always let you feel the sweetness of this love, he does this in order to render you more despicable and humble in your own eyes. You should not fail, however, for this reason, to turn to his goodness with every confidence. Because what was his purpose in taking on this loving condition of a child, if not to provoke our loving him with confidence, and to lovingly confide in him?

"Stay very close to the crib of this most beautiful child. . . . Have a great love for this heavenly child, respectful in the familiarity you will gain with him through prayer, and totally delighted in the joy of feeling the holy aspirations and effects of belonging totally to him."[2]

*Lord, lead me each day to a closer relationship with you, and help me to appreciate your coming among us as a little child. Amen.*

# *Comfort*

Isaiah 61:1-2: "The spirit of the Lord G<small>OD</small> is upon me, because the L<small>ORD</small> has anointed me; he has sent me . . . to comfort all who mourn. . . ."[1]

Acts 9:31: "Meanwhile the church . . . had peace and was built up. Living in the fear of the Lord and in the comfort of the Holy Spirit. . . ."[2]

*I have no trouble fearing the Lord, but where is the comfort of the Holy Spirit? I worry that my troubles are too great for God.*

Padre Pio's assurance: "May Jesus comfort and bless you! Why are you so sad? . . . Dispel all these childish fears which are aroused by the enemy of every good. Take comfort in the Lord and let yourself be transported by him, like a little ship in the middle of the ocean. Therefore, cast aside that silly and crazy worry, calm your soul, and don't you break my heart. I bless you."[3]

"May the infant Jesus bless you, comfort you, reward you for what you are bearing for love of him, and make you holy. . . . Let the trials be great; he who sends them to you is greater and more provident."[4]

*By your grace, Lord, I will accept the trials you send me, knowing that your comfort and strength will accompany them, so that they do not overwhelm me. Thank you. Amen.*

# Comparison

Mark 2:16-17: "When the scribes of the Pharisees saw that he was eating with sinners and tax collectors, they said to his disciples, 'Why does he eat with tax collectors and sinners?' When Jesus heard this, he said to them, 'Those who are well have no need of a physician, but those who are sick; I have come to call not the righteous but sinners.' "[1]

*But when I compare myself to others, I feel so inferior, so hopelessly imperfect and sinful. God can't possibly want to "call" me.*

Padre Pio's assurance: "Do not give too much importance to what the enemy and your imagination suggest to you. . . ."[2]

"Do you know what religion is? It is the academy of perfection in which each soul must learn to allow itself to be handled, planed, and smoothed by the divine Spirit, when he also acts as a doctor of our souls so that, having been well-planed and smoothed, they can be united and joined to the will of God.

"Religion is a hospital for the spiritually ill who wish to be cured, and in order to achieve this, they submit themselves to . . . some probing, surgical instruments, fire, and all the pains of medicine."[3]

*How merciful you are, Lord, to go to all this trouble to save me. I submit myself, now and forever, to the fire of your divine medicine. Amen.*

# *Condemnation of Self*

John 3:17-18: "Indeed, God did not send the Son into the world to condemn the world, but in order that the world might be saved through him. Those who believe in him are not condemned; but those who do not believe are condemned already, because they have not believed in the name of the only Son of God."[1]

*But I do believe in the name of the Lord, and look at how I still stumble through life, always making mistakes, never holy enough.*

Padre Pio's assurance: "You are very strange if you are not pleased with the fact that your beautiful tree is firm and strongly and deeply rooted in the earth. Not only that, but you expect not even a leaf to be blown about by the wind.

"Make positive acts of love for God and confidence in his goodness, in order to divert your attention."[2]

"Come on, if you were to judge people, and if God were to judge people as you usually judge yourself, everyone would perish, and the very angels would have to be put out of paradise!

"Take heart and do not fear. Jesus is with you."[3]

*Forgive my impatience and ingratitude toward what you are doing in me. Forgive me for expecting perfection from myself and others. Amen.*

# Confidence in God

Proverbs 3:26: ". . . for the LORD will be your confidence / and will keep your foot from being caught."[1]

Hebrews 3:6: "Christ, however, was faithful over God's house as a son, and we are his house if we hold firm the confidence and the pride that belong to hope."[2]

*But in the middle of my trials, how can I have confidence in God?*

Padre Pio's assurance: "I know from my own experience that the best way to avoid falling is to lean on the cross of Jesus, with confidence in him alone who for our salvation desired to be nailed to it."[3]

"Courage then, courage all the time, for the Lord has never been so close to you as he has been, and still is, in this trial.

"May this knowledge fill you and hearten you continually with fresh courage to face up to all the trials. . . . Jesus, who is infinitely merciful, will not fail to give you, now and then, a respite from the trial he has sent you. He is so good that he will never allow you to give in."[4]

"Arm yourself with the beautiful virtue of trust in the Lord and take heed of the assurances which God gives you through me."[5]

*Help me to always practice confidence in you, God, no matter what happens. Amen.*

# Consolation

2 Corinthians 1:5: "For just as the sufferings of Christ are abundant for us, so also our consolation is abundant through Christ."[1]

*But often I'd rather focus on my problems, ignoring God's consolation.*

Padre Pio's assurance: "I do not know when my own afflictions will end, but praise be to Jesus who, as Master and King of my heart, never ceases to console me."[2]

"I have no means of thanking our dear Jesus who gives me such strength and courage to bear not only the many ailments he sends me, but even the continual temptations which he in fact permits and which grow more numerous day by day. . . . I must admit, however, that I am happy even in the midst of these afflictions because almost every day our good Jesus also makes me taste great sweetness."[3]

"Oh, at this moment when I still feel almost all of this sweetness, if I could only bury within my heart these consolations, I should certainly be in paradise!"[4]

"What a consolation it is to know almost with certainty that one possesses Jesus."[5]

*Dear God, when I would rather focus on my afflictions, help me, instead, to thank you for the many consolations you daily give me. Amen.*

Every day, Padre Pio said many Rosaries for suffering souls, and he advised others to ask the Mother of God for her intercession. "Let us invariably unite with this dear Mother; with her, close to Jesus" (*Letters, Volume I*).

# Contemplation

Luke 10:42: ". . . there is need of only one thing [contemplating Jesus]."[1]

Romans 8:26: "Likewise the Spirit helps us in our weakness; for we do not know how to pray as we ought, but that very Spirit intercedes with sighs too deep for words."[2]

*But when I try to contemplate the Lord, my spirit sees only darkness.*

Padre Pio's assurance: "But if the spirit is also enveloped in darkness, within this fog there is a clear, pure, delightful, divine, and delicate light. . . . You cannot discern this light, but it is none the less true that precisely this light strengthens and invigorates you in the service and persevering love of the Lord.

"It is this light, moreover, which is for you and for your soul the beginning of contemplation. You cannot fully achieve this contemplation until you have submitted humbly to the purification of the senses."[3]

"Yet, who would believe that this light, which in the beginning invades the soul with such desolation and pain, is later to raise it up to mystical and transforming union?"[4]

"Remember that one thing only is necessary: To be close to Jesus."[5]

*Purify me, Lord, so that my spirit may contemplate you always. Amen.*

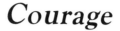

# Courage

Psalm 27:14: "Wait for the LORD; / be strong, and let your heart take courage; / wait for the LORD!"[1]

*But many times I have neither courage nor patience.*

Padre Pio's assurance: "You have every reason to be frightened when you measure the trial by your own strength, but the knowledge that Jesus never leaves you even for an instant should bring you the greatest consolation. God himself tells us that he is with those who are afflicted and in distress: 'I will be with them in trouble.'[2] He even comes down to dry their tears. Be comforted, then, by the delightful thought that after such pitch darkness, the beautiful noonday sun will shine."[3]

"Live joyfully and courageously and don't extinguish the Spirit of the Lord within you."[4]

"Rest assured that the more a soul is pleasing to God, the more it must be tried. Therefore, courage and go forward always. Let us do good while we still have time, and we will render glory to our heavenly Father, sanctify ourselves, and give good example to others."[5]

*Lord, when I'd rather worry because it seems you're not doing anything, when I'd rather hide from my troubles and fears than face them, grant me patience to wait for you, and courage to stand up to trials. Amen.*

# *Cross*

Mark 8:34: "If any want to become my followers, let them deny themselves and take up their cross and follow me."[1]

*But the weight of my cross threatens to crush me.*

Padre Pio's assurance: "We don't reach salvation without crossing the stormy sea, continually threatened with disaster. Calvary is the hill of the saints, but from there we pass on to another mountain [heaven].

"But when will this day come? When will we sing the hymn of victory over all our enemies? When will we be allowed to intone the alleluia? Alas, it is still far off. Justice has not yet been done. Praise be to God and may his justice be done!"[2]

"Beneath the cross one learns to love. . . ."[3]

"I know from my own experience that the best way to avoid falling is to lean on the cross of Jesus, with confidence in him alone who for our salvation desired to be nailed to it."[4]

"The Lord loads us and sets us free from our load, for when he bestows a cross on one of his chosen ones, he strengthens that soul to such an extent that by bearing the weight of this cross he is relieved of it."[5]

*Lord, even though my cross threatens to crush me, please teach me to willingly accept it and to lean on you with confidence. Amen.*

# *Dangers*

Romans 8:35, 37: "Who will separate us from the love of Christ? Will hardship, or distress, or persecution, or famine, or nakedness, or peril, or sword? . . . No, in all these things we are more than conquerors through him who loved us."[1]

*But I see great danger lurking ahead of me.*

Padre Pio's assurance: "Always look ahead without troubling too much in reflecting on the dangers you see at a distance. These seem to you to be an enormous army, but they are nothing, only pruned willow trees."[2]

"Convince yourselves that you belong to Jesus, and that the storm which Satan blows against you cannot harm you at all. Therefore, do not fear. Jesus is more powerful than all hell, and at the invocation of his holy name, all knees in heaven, earth, and hell bend, to the consolation of the good and the terror of the wicked."[3]

"Let Satan wage war either directly by his evil promptings, or indirectly by means of the world and our own corrupt nature. . . . it doesn't matter, for he can achieve nothing against your soul, which Jesus has now clasped to himself and sustains in a mysterious manner. . . ."[4]

*Thank you, Lord, for your constant protection. No matter what dangers I see waiting up ahead, help me to always face life with trust in you. Amen.*

# *Death*

Psalm 116:15: "Precious in the sight of the LORD is the death of his faithful ones."[1]

Romans 6:5: "For if we have been united with him in a death like his, we will certainly be united with him in a resurrection like his."[2]

Isaiah 25:7: ". . . he will swallow up death forever."[3]

*But when a loved one dies, nothing can comfort me.*

Padre Pio's assurance: "This present life is given to us in order to acquire the eternal, and due to a lack of reflection, we base our affections on that which pertains to this world through which we are passing, so that when we have to leave it, we are frightened and agitated. In order to live happily while on pilgrimage, we must keep before our eyes the hope of arriving at our homeland where we will stay for eternity, and in the meantime we should believe this firmly. Because given that it is God who calls us to himself, he watches how we make our way to him, and will never permit anything to happen to us that is not for our greater good."[4]

*When loved ones die, Lord, help me to focus on the happiness they experience in heaven with you, rather than on my sorrow over losing them. Thank you. Amen.*

# Little Defects

Psalm 19:12: "But who can detect their errors? / Clear me from hidden faults."[1]

*But when I ask God to cleanse and perfect me, I still have defects.*

Padre Pio's assurance: "Don't philosophize on your defects. . . ."[2]

"Don't let these little imperfections discourage you. Try to be always watchful in order to avoid sin, but when you see that you fail in some way, don't become lost in useless complaining, but bend your knees before God; be embarrassed at your scarce fidelity; humble yourself greatly; ask our Lord's pardon; propose to be more watchful in the future; and then get up immediately and carry on. . . ."[3]

"Walk with simplicity in the ways of the Lord and do not torment your spirit. You must hate your faults, but with a quiet hate, not troublesome and restless. We must be patient with them and gain from them through holy humility."[4]

"It is equally true that God allows the master spies — venial sins and imperfections — to circulate freely in his kingdom, but this is merely to show us that, without him, we should be a prey for our enemies."[5]

*When I fail, Lord, help me to ask forgiveness, then to go forward and not dwell on my faults. Through them, help me to gain patience and humility. Amen.*

# *Delight*

Proverbs 8:30-31: ". . . I was daily his delight, / rejoicing before him always, / rejoicing in his inhabited world and delighting in the human race."[1]

*But how can I rejoice when misery darkens my heart and mind?*

Padre Pio's assurance: "What soul, to whom Jesus has given himself as its inheritance, can be unhappy? Is he not the same Jesus who is the delight of the angels? . . . Let us spend the whole of our lives giving thanks to the divine Father who, in an excess of love for us, sent his only begotten Son and our most sweet lover. Protected, or rather, covered and defended, by the uniform of this dear Lord, let us stand before him and pray with the humility of the creature and the confidence and freedom of the child. And given that he loves to delight in the children of humans, let nothing in the world distract us from delighting in him and contemplating his grandeur and infinite titles, by which he has a right to our praises and love. Let us pray to him that he be generous, as usual, with his divine help, so that through us his holy name may be greatly praised and blessed. So that we, too, can say in truth, with our heavenly Mother, 'My soul magnifies the Lord, and my spirit rejoices in God my Savior.' "[2]

*Grant me the grace to delight in you always, Lord, like a child, like your most holy Mother. Amen.*

# Desires

1 Peter 2:2: "Like newborn infants, long for the pure, spiritual milk, so that by it you may grow into salvation. . . ."[1]

Hebrews 11:16: "But as it is, they desire a better country, that is, a heavenly one."[2]

*But too many times worldly desires overpower my desire to love God.*

Padre Pio's assurance: "We sometimes desire to be good angels, and we neglect to be good people. Our imperfection must accompany us to the coffin, and we cannot reach this without the earth. We shouldn't sleep there nor turn around, given that we are like little chickens, without the wings, however. Little by little we die to physical life, and this is an ordinary law held by providence."[3]

"Let us be content with walking with our feet on the ground, as being in the wide open sea makes us dizzy and causes convulsions. Let us stay at the feet of the divine Master with Mary Magdalene."[4]

"Oh how burdensome this mortal life is to the children of God. But the next life, which the mercy of the Lord will be pleased to grant us, will be more than we could desire."[5]

*Lord, make my desire to love you always overpower my worldly desires, and use me to serve you by serving those around me. Amen.*

# *Desolation*

Luke 1:78-79: "By the tender mercy of our God, / the dawn from on high will break upon us, / to give light to those who sit in darkness and in the shadow of death, / to guide our feet into the way of peace."[1]

*But if Christ came to give light, why does darkness still surround me?*

Padre Pio's assurance: ". . . the state of your soul is one of desolation or holy spiritual suffering. . . . The darkness that surrounds the sky of your soul is light, and you do well to say you see nothing, and that you find yourself in the midst of a burning bush. The bush burns, the air fills with clouds, and your soul neither sees nor understands anything. But God speaks just the same and is present to the soul. . . ."[2]

"The most beautiful credo is that pronounced in darkness, in times of sacrifice, and when one has to make a great effort to do this."[3]

"In conclusion, rest assured and be happy because God is pleased with you and finds his peaceful dwelling place within you. Temptations, discomfort, and restlessness are the merchandise offered by the enemy, but you reject them, so it does no harm. Remember this: That if the devil makes a din, he is still outside and not inside at all."[4]

*Even when desolation surrounds me, Lord, I will trust in you. Amen.*

# Devotion Through Humble and Suffering Prayer

Hebrews 5:7: "In the days of his flesh, Jesus offered up prayers and supplications, with loud cries and tears, to the one who was able to save him from death, and he was heard because of his reverent submission."[1]

*Jesus is God, so of course our Father listens to him. But does he listen to me?*

Padre Pio's assurance: "No matter how great the trial . . . never lose heart. Have recourse, with more childlike trust, to Jesus who will never be able to resist bestowing on you some little solace and comfort. Turn to him at all times, even when the devil tries to cast a pall over your life by showing you your sins. Lift up your voice loudly to Jesus and let it express your spiritual humility, your heartfelt contrition, and your vocal prayer.

"It is impossible for God not to welcome these demonstrations of goodwill and not to give way and surrender to you. It is true that God's power triumphs over everything, but humble and suffering prayer prevails over God himself. It stops his hand, extinguishes his lightning, disarms him, vanquishes and placates him, and makes him almost a dependent and a friend."[2]

*Lord, help me to always pray, even when my sins mock me. Then, like Jesus, "with loud cries and tears," I will thank and praise you for your unending love. Amen.*

Not only did Padre Pio urge people to read the Bible and other holy books, he also read them himself. "Continue with your spiritual reading, because it is God who speaks to the soul through the correct reading of those books" (*Letters, Volume III*).

# *Distractions*

1 Thessalonians 5:17: " . . . pray without ceasing."[1]

*But every time I try to pray, something distracts and interrupts me. I worry that God will give up on me.*

Padre Pio's assurance: "Do not be surprised at your distractions and spiritual aridity. This derives partly from the senses and partly from your heart which is not entirely under your control. But, your courage which God granted you is irremovable and constantly determined. Therefore, live tranquilly. You must not be anxious, however long this evil lasts.

"Live humbly; be docile and in love with your heavenly spouse. Do not be upset by any infirmities and weaknesses into which you could fall. . . . Because just as one often falls without realizing it, in the same way, without realizing it, we will arise."[2]

"Don't upset yourself over this, but humbly and frankly confess before God what you noticed, and place it at the sweet mercy of him who sustains those who fall without malice, so that they do not suffer any harm. He picks them up so sweetly, that they do not realize they have fallen because the hand of God sustained them in their fall. . . ."[3]

*Lord, teach me to be patient with myself, so that, during prayer, I do not allow those inevitable distractions to discourage me. Amen.*

# *Divine Artist*

Romans 9:21: "Has the potter no right over the clay, to make out of the same lump one object for special use and another for ordinary use?"[1]

*Yes, God has all rights over me, but why does it sometimes seem as if he is trying to destroy me with adversity?*

Padre Pio's assurance: "With repeated blows of the chisel and diligent smoothing, the divine artist wants to prepare the stones with which to construct the eternal edifice."[2]

"Therefore, let God be thanked for treating you as a soul chosen to follow Jesus closely up the hill of Calvary. . . . It is not abandonment but love that the most sweet Savior is showing you. It is not true at all that you offend God in that state [of suffering]. . . . Therefore, if you don't offend God at all, but rather you love him in that state desired by him, why should you be sorry? Why should you afflict yourself? Therefore, undertake your salvation on the cross. Stretch yourself out on it and be patient with yourself, because, in your patience, as the divine Master tells us, you will possess your soul.[3] And the less this possession is mixed up with haste and restlessness, the more stable it will be."[4]

*Lord, I accept the cross you have chosen for me, and I thank you. Grant me the grace to carry it with patience and love, for you. Amen.*

# Domestic Life

Psalm 61:8: "So I will always sing praises to your name, / as I pay my vows day after day."[1]

*But how am I to grow in grace and holiness if I'm stuck in this humdrum way of life with all its demands and tedious tasks?*

Padre Pio's assurance: "Therefore, live tranquilly, follow the path on which the Lord has placed you and, in a holy manner. . . . So just like a bee who is carefully making the honey of holy devout practices, also make the wax of domestic affairs, because if the former brings with it a sweetness pleasing to Christ . . . the latter superabounds with glory for him because it serves to make lighted candles for the edification of one's neighbor."[2]

"But remember that the mind can quite well be elevated to God while the body attends to material matters. Therefore, don't distress yourself if you are unable to carry out your usual spiritual exercises due to a great deal of work. Endeavor, without wearying yourself, to do what you can, and Jesus, who looks into the depths of the heart, will be pleased with you."[3]

"We are not all called to the same state, and the Holy Spirit doesn't work in all souls in the same way. He blows as he wills and where he wills."[4]

*Lord, help me to appreciate my state in life, and to worship, love, and give glory to you through the carrying out of my daily tasks. Amen.*

# *Dryness of Spirit*

Isaiah 35:6-7: "For waters shall break forth in the wilderness, / and streams in the desert; / the burning sand shall become a pool, / and the thirsty ground springs of water."[1]

*But I can't believe that my dryness of spirit, my lack of enthusiasm about praying, will ever go away or lead to any good.*

Padre Pio's assurance: "You will please God in a supreme manner by not failing to carry out your devout practices in times of interior aridity and languor which often return to you. Because if you don't want to serve and love God simply for love of him, and as the service we render him amidst the sufferings of aridity is more pleasing to him than that which we render him amidst sweetness, we must likewise receive them willingly, at least with our superior will. . . ."[2]

"Don't worry about your spirit, because it is by no means true that you have lost the path. The one on which you are walking is the true and safe way, and will lead you to the port of salvation.

"Don't be upset by aridity . . . [remember] what the divine Master said, 'Blessed are the poor in spirit, for theirs is the kingdom of heaven.' "[3]

*Thank you, Lord, that even when the act of praying burdens my dry spirit, you are there, leading me, encouraging me. Onward, Lord. Amen.*

# Encouragement

1 Thessalonians 5:14: "And we urge you, beloved, to admonish the idlers, encourage the faint hearted, help the weak, be patient with all of them."[1]

*But how can I encourage anyone when I myself need encouragement?*

Padre Pio's assurance: "Do not be discouraged or frightened by your miseries and weaknesses, because God has seen even worse sins in you, and, by his mercy did not reject you. God does not reject poor sinners, and he will not reject you either, but on the contrary, he will grant you his grace, and will erect the throne of his glory on your misery and vileness. Therefore, do not fear and do not be anxious anymore about the doubts of your conscience because fear is in vain and diabolical. Don't worry if your brothers and sisters don't want to listen to you; correct them always and don't worry about anything else."[2]

"Lift up your heart. Do not become discouraged in the face of the trials to which divine mercy wishes to subject you. He wants to test and strengthen you once again at the school of sacrifice and suffering. Do not become discouraged. Pray with humility, and remember the calm after the rain; after the darkness, light; after the storm and the turmoil, placid quiet."[3]

*Lord, thank you for the encouragement. Help me to always pass it on to others, assuring them of the calm that will follow their storm. Amen.*

# *Enemy*

Luke 1:72-74: "Thus he . . . has remembered his holy covenant . . . to grant us that we, being rescued from the hands of our enemies, might serve him without fear, in holiness and righteousness before him all our days."[1]

*But sometimes I don't feel as if God has rescued me from my enemies.*

Padre Pio's assurance: "The devil continues to make war on me and unfortunately shows no sign of admitting defeat. In the first days during which I was put to the test, I confess that I was weak and became almost melancholy, but then by degrees this melancholy feeling passed, and I began to feel somewhat relieved. Later, when I prayed at the feet of Jesus, I seemed to feel no trace of the burden entailed in trying to overcome myself when tempted, or of the chagrin occasioned by my troubles.

"Dear God! Even in ascending the altar I experience these attacks [of the enemy], but I have Jesus with me, and what should I fear?"[2]

"May Jesus comfort you in all your afflictions; may he sustain you in dangers, watch over you always with his grace, indicate the safe path that leads to eternal salvation, and may he render you always dearer to his divine heart and always more worthy of paradise."[3]

*Lord, with you always by my side, I have nothing to fear. I will trust you to defend me from my enemies, even from those within. Amen.*

# *Eternal Life*

John 17:24: "Father, I desire that those also, whom you have given me, may be with me where I am, to see my glory [in eternity], which you have given me because you loved me before the foundation of the world."[1]

*But I have done nothing to deserve eternal life with God.*

Padre Pio's assurance: "We must ask the Spirit, the Comforter, to . . . make us increasingly aware of the excellence of our Christian vocation. The fact of having been chosen, having been elected among innumerable others, and knowing that without any merit on our part, this choice, this election was decided by God from all eternity, 'before the foundation of the world,'[2] for the sole reason that we might be his in time and in eternity, is such a great and at the same time such an enchanting mystery that the soul, even though it understands so little of all this, cannot but melt away with love.

"Secondly, let us pray that he may enlighten us more and more as to the immensity of the eternal inheritance which has been reserved for us by the goodness of the heavenly Father. May our discernment of this mystery turn our hearts away from earthly goods and make us eager to arrive at our heavenly home."[3]

*Lord, thank you for the gift of eternal life. Amen.*

# *Eucharist*

Matthew 6:11: "Give us this day our daily bread."[1]

*But bread isn't enough; food isn't enough. I need more. I need something to fill the dark, hungry emptiness inside my heart and soul.*

Padre Pio's assurance: "Well, then, his [Christ's] immense love, that same love that induced him to leave the bosom of his eternal Father in order to come on earth and take upon himself our fragility and our debts and satisfy the divine justice for us, found an admirable means in which he showed us his exceedingly great love for us. What means was this? Oh, for the love of heaven, let us understand what our good Master asked the Father immediately after he had offered our will to him. In his own name and in ours he asked him also, 'Give us this day our daily bread.'[2]

"But what bread is this? In Jesus' request here, failing a better interpretation, I recognize primarily the Eucharist. Oh, the exceeding humility of this Man-God! He is one with the Father, he is the love and delight of the eternal parent. Although he knew that everything he would do on earth would be pleasing and would be ratified by his Father in heaven, he asked leave to remain with us!"[3]

*Lord, thank you for your Body and Blood, the Eucharist, broken for us — for me. I need nothing more. Amen.*

# *Failings*

Romans 7:21-24: "So I find it to be a law that when I want to do what is good, evil lies close at hand. For I delight in the law of God in my inmost self, but I see in my members another law at war with the law of my mind, making me captive to the law of sin that dwells in my members. Wretched man that I am! Who will rescue me from this body of death?"[1]

*Too often I echo those verses as my sinful nature threatens to take over.*

Padre Pio's assurance: "Convince yourselves that failings and little flights of the passions are inevitable as long as we are in this life. . . ."[2]

"We must resign ourselves to what we have inherited from our ancestors Adam and Eve. Self-love never dies before we do, but it will accompany us to the tomb. Dear God, what unhappiness this is for us, poor children of Eve! We must always feel the sensitive assaults of the passions, as long as we are in this miserable exile. But what of it? Should we perhaps become discouraged and renounce the life of heaven? No, let us take heart. It is sufficient for us not to consent with our deliberate will; deliberate, firm, and sustained."[3]

*Lord, when my failings discourage me, help me to echo Saint Paul when he said, "Who will rescue me from this body of death? Thanks be to God through Jesus Christ our Lord!"[4] Amen.*

# *Faith*

1 Peter 5:8: ". . . keep alert. Like a roaring lion your adversary the devil prowls around, looking for someone to devour."[1]

*But when evil threatens me, my mind clouds, my soul quakes, and my faith in God seems to vanish.*

Padre Pio's assurance: "Be steadfast and firm in your faith, and be on the alert, for in this way you will avoid all the evil snares of the enemy. This is precisely the warning given us by the prince of the Apostles, Saint Peter [in the scripture above].For our greater encouragement, he adds, 'Resist him, steadfast in your faith, for you know that your brothers and sisters in all the world are undergoing the same kinds of suffering.'[2]

"Yes, renew . . . your faith in the promises of eternal life which our most sweet Jesus makes to those who fight energetically and courageously. You should be encouraged and comforted by the knowledge that we are not alone in our sufferings, for all the followers of the Nazarene scattered throughout the world suffer in the same manner and are all exposed like ourselves to the trials and tribulations of life."[3]

*Lord, thank you that I am never alone in my sufferings, and that the help you give to others during their trials you will give to me, too. Amen.*

Padre Pio daily meditated on and paid homage to Christ crucified. "Beneath the cross one learns to love" (*Letters, Volume I*).

# *Family: Your Boat*

Mark 4:37-39: ". . . waves beat into the boat, so that the boat was already being swamped. But he [Jesus] was . . . asleep on the cushion; and they woke him up and said to him, '. . . do you not care that we are perishing?' "[1]

*When troubles whip at our family, God sometimes seems to sleep, and I want to give up, abandon ship.*

Padre Pio's assurance: ". . . stay in the boat in which our Lord has placed you, and let the storm come. You will not perish. It appears to you that Jesus is sleeping, but let it be so. Don't you know that if he sleeps, his heart vigilantly watches over you? Let him sleep, but at the right time, he will awaken to restore your calm.

"Scripture tells us that dearest Saint Peter [when walking on the water] was frightened. Trembling, he exclaimed, 'Oh, Lord, save me!' And our Lord, taking him by the hand, replied, 'You of little faith, why did you doubt?'[2] . . . You are walking on the sea, and you find the wind and waves, but isn't it enough to be with Jesus? . . . But if fear takes you by surprise, cry, 'Oh, Lord, save me!' He will stretch out his hand to you. Hold onto it tightly, and joyfully walk on the stormy sea of life."[3]

*I promise to stay in my "boat," Lord, knowing that you will buoy me up. Thank you for my family. Always use me to love and help them. Amen.*

# *Father God*

Luke 21:18: "But not a hair of your head will perish."[1]

*How can I know for sure that nothing and no one will harm me?*

Padre Pio's assurance: ". . . keep imprinted on your soul that God is our Father. So what have you to fear while you are the child of such a Father, through whose providence not even a single hair will fall from your head?[2] In truth, it is amazing that, as we are children of such a Father, we can and do have any other thought except that of serving him. Assist and take care of your soul and family as he wishes, and don't worry about anything else, because if you do this, you will see that Jesus will take care of you. . . . The book of Wisdom tells us that, 'It is your providence, O Father, that steers its [our] course, because you have given it [us] a path in the sea, and a safe way through the waves' "[3]

"If God did not abandon you in the past, how can he abandon you in the future, when you want to be his from now on, even more so than you did in the past?"[4]

*Father God, when I doubt your protection and love for me, remind me of how you cared for me in the past, and that you will continue to care for me in the future, no matter what. Thank you. Amen.*

# *Fear*

Psalm 23:4: "Even though I walk through the darkest valley, I fear no evil; for you are with me; your rod and your staff — they comfort me."[1]

*But even though I know this, why does fear still haunt me?*

Padre Pio's assurance: "If we earnestly endeavor to love Jesus, this alone will drive all fear from our hearts, and the soul will find that instead of walking in the Lord's paths, it is flying."[2]

"As regards your fear of offending God and of not knowing how to please him, I beseech you to calm your anxiety. Believe the assurances of authority which tells you, on behalf of God, that however you act, as long as you do not clearly see your actions to be contrary to the law of God and the established authorities, Jesus is always pleased with you, when your actions are directed for the glory of God.

"With this safe guide, you must act without questioning; you must go forward without heeding the voice of your fears. . . . I don't say you are not to 'hear' them, because you can't help this, but you mustn't worry about them."[3]

*Lord, help me to "earnestly endeavor" to love you and to direct all my actions for your glory, so that I will always please you, and so that all my fears will vanish. Amen.*

# *Food of the Angels*

Matthew 26:26: "Take, eat; this is my body."[1]

*But some people laugh at my faith in the Eucharist.*

Padre Pio's assurance: "Never fail to eat the food of the angels. You will receive many temptations from the enemy, who is not unaware of the benefit your soul receives from this food, and which many others receive through you, but you must not be frightened. Jesus promised that he will continue to assist you."[2]

"If you are not granted the ability to stay a long time in prayer, reading, etc., you must not be discouraged. As long as you receive Jesus in the Blessed Sacrament every morning, you must consider yourself extremely fortunate."[3]

"Fly in spirit before the tabernacle when you cannot go there with the body, and there express your ardent desires. . . . Embrace the Beloved of souls, better than if you had been able to receive him in Sacrament."[4]

" 'Give us this day our daily bread.'[5] Always give us Jesus during our brief stay in this land of exile. Give him to us and grant that we may be increasingly worthy to welcome him into our hearts."[6]

*Lord, always draw me to your table and give me the "food of the angels." Use it to transform me into your faithful, loving servant. Amen.*

# *Footsteps of God*

Psalm 17:5: "My steps have held fast to your paths; my feet have not slipped."[1]

*But how can I recognize God's paths, and how can I not slip?*

Padre Pio's assurance: "Let us ascend Calvary, laden with the cross, without tiring, and let us firmly believe that our ascent will lead us to the heavenly vision of our most sweet Savior.

"Therefore, let us draw away, step by step, from earthly affections, and let us aspire to the happiness prepared for us. And if we desire to reach the blessed Sion [heaven] soon, we must banish all uneasiness and worry — because they are contrary to the free workings of the Holy Spirit — by bearing spiritual and temporal tribulations, wherever they come from."[2]

"Let us take courage at the consoling thought that, after the climb to Calvary, we will ascend even higher, without any effort on our part, to the holy mount of God, the heavenly Jerusalem. By divine goodness we are already halfway up the mount of suffering because we are absolutely determined to serve and love this divine goodness well."[3]

*Lord, help me to follow you to Calvary by accepting my crosses, and keep my gaze always fixed on you. Amen.*

# *Forgive With Love*

Colossians 3:13-14: "Bear with one another and, if anyone has a complaint against another, forgive each other. . . . Above all, clothe yourselves with love, which binds everything together in perfect harmony."[1]

*But sometimes I can't forgive; the wounds hurt too much. And I certainly can't forgive with love.*

Padre Pio's assurance: "Saint Paul [in the above scripture] expects you to bear with all the vexatious behavior of others and to forgive them. . . . This great saint, however, sets greater store by love than by all the rest of the virtues, and hence he . . . expects it to be present in all we do. . . ."[2]

"He wants us to love, and with good reason, for it might well be that we bear patiently with the defects of those around us and even forgive them when they offend us, but all this may be of no value if it is done without love, which is the queen of virtues and includes all the others.

". . . Let us love and practice charity, as this is our divine Master's precept. We shall be distinguished from the unbelievers by our loving and charitable behavior. . . . If we keep our love for one another, the beautiful peace of Jesus will invariably triumph joyfully in our hearts."[3]

*Lord, no matter how much or how often others hurt me, help me to forgive them — and to do it with love. Amen.*

# *Freedom in God's Word, God's Will*

John 8:31-32: "Then Jesus said to the Jews who had believed in him, 'If you continue in my word, you are truly my disciples; and you will know the truth, and the truth will make you free.' "[1]

*God's word, God's will — I want to continue in it, but how can I when I have failed to recognize and obey it?*

Padre Pio's assurance: "I give heartfelt thanks to the heavenly Father, through his most beloved Son, Jesus, for all those graces which he scattered and continually scatters in your soul, despite your every unworthiness. How good the Lord is to everyone; but he is even more so to those who have a true and sincere desire to please him in everything. . . .

"You, too, must learn to more greatly recognize and adore divine will in all the events of life. Often repeat the divine words of our dearest Master: '*Fiat voluntas Dei sicut in coelo et in terra* [Your will be done, on earth as it is in heaven].'[2] Yes, let this beautiful exclamation always be in your heart and on your lips. . . . Say it in times of affliction; say it in times of temptation. . . . Say it again when you feel yourself submerged in the ocean of love for Jesus; it will be your anchor and salvation."[3]

*Lord, help me to recognize and follow your word — your will — in all aspects of my life, because in your will, I find true freedom. Amen.*

# *Friend in the Dark*

Isaiah 41:8-10: "But you . . . whom I have chosen, / the offspring of Abraham, my friend . . . do not fear, for I am with you. . . ."[1]

John 8:12: "I am the light of the world."[2]

*But if Jesus is the light of the world, why does the darkness in my soul keep me from seeing his light and the path he wants me to follow?*

Padre Pio's assurance: "Don't be bewildered if the night becomes deeper and darker for you. Don't be frightened if you are unable to see, with the eyes of the body, the serene sky that surrounds your soul.

"A lively faith, blind belief, and complete adherence to the authorities constituted by God over you, this is the light . . . that led the Magi to adore the newly born Messiah.[3] . . . And this light . . . also illuminates your soul and directs your footsteps so that you do not stumble. It fortifies your spirit with divine affection. Without the soul's being aware of it, it continually advances towards the eternal goal. You neither see it nor understand it, but this is not necessary. . . . Believe that [the eternal] Sun shines in your soul, and it is precisely that Sun about which the prophet of God sang, 'In your light, we see light.' "[4]

*Lord and Friend, even when darkness surrounds my soul and I can't see your light, I will trust in you, "the light of the world."[5] Amen.*

# *Future/Eternity*

1 Corinthians 15:51-53: ". . . we will all be changed, in a moment, in the twinkling of an eye, at the last trumpet. . . . For this perishable body must put on imperishability, and this mortal body must put on immortality."[1]

*But what should I do in the meantime? So many troubles try to tear me apart. Worry and fear clog my head and heart.*

Padre Pio's assurance: "The children of God should have very little interest in living these short moments which pass, as long as they live for eternity in the glory of God. Consider that you are already on the road to eternity; you have already placed one foot there. And as long as this eternity is happy for you, why do you worry if these transitory moments cause you to suffer?"[2]

"Furthermore, try to always guard these two virtues in your heart: Sweetness towards your neighbor and loving humility towards God. And I hope you will succeed in this because this God who has taken you by the hand in order to bring you to himself will never abandon you until you are assured of his eternal tabernacle."[3]

*Lord, thank you for holding my hand. Continue to lead me through this life's troubles as well as its joys. Without you, I would never make it to heaven, let alone through each day here on earth. Amen.*

# Gifts of God

1 Corinthians 4:7: "What do you have that you did not receive? And if you received it, why do you boast as if it were not a gift?"[1]

James 1:17: "Every generous act of giving, with every perfect gift, is from above, coming down from the Father of lights. . . ."[2]

*Does that mean I should credit God for even my motivation to do good?*

Padre Pio's assurance: "You should strive to ask God constantly to be preserved from vice, for 'every perfect gift is from above, coming down from the Father of lights.'[3] Open wide your heart to trust in God, always bearing in mind that all that is good in you is a pure gift of the heavenly bridegroom's supreme bounty.

"You should impress on your mind, engrave deeply in your heart, and be convinced that none is good except God,[4] and that all we have is nothing.

"If the enemy attacks you on the score of the holiness of your life, shout in his face, 'My holiness is not an effect of my own spirit, but it is the Spirit of God who sanctifies me. This is a gift from God, a talent lent to me by my spouse, so that I can trade with it and, when the time comes, give him an exact account of the profit I have gained.' "[5]

*Lord, when tempted to credit myself for any good I do, remind me that all good gifts — including my talent and motivation — come from you. Amen.*

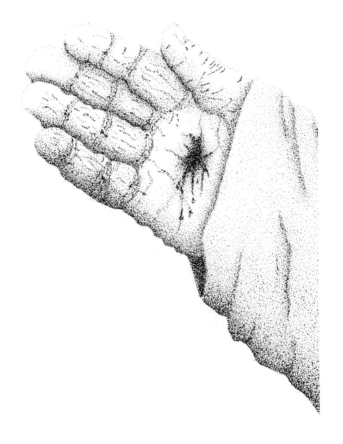

From 1918 until just before his death in 1968, Padre Pio bore the five bleeding wounds of Christ crucified. "When we suffer, Jesus is closer to us" (*Letters, Volume I*).

# God's Spirit

Romans 8:13: "For if you live according to the flesh, you will die; but if by the Spirit you put to death the deeds of the body, you will live."[1]

*But won't that hurt?*

Padre Pio's assurance: "Make this resolution: either to die or be cured. And as you don't want to die spiritually, try to be healed perfectly. And in order to be healed, desire to bear the treatment and correction of the divine doctor [the Holy Spirit], and beseech him not to spare you in anything in order to save you."[2]

"Live calmly and do not worry excessively, because in order to work more freely in us, the Holy Spirit needs tranquillity and calm. And for you, every anxious thought is a mistake, as you have no reason to fear. It is the Lord who works within you, and you must do nothing except leave the door of your heart wide open so that he might work as he pleases."[3]

"Throw yourself confidently into the arms of the heavenly Father with childlike trust and open wide your heart to the charism of the Holy Spirit, who is only waiting for a sign from you in order to enrich you."[4]

*Heavenly Father, by the power of your Holy Spirit, transform me — even if it hurts — into the person you want me to be. Amen.*

# *Gratitude*

1 Peter 2:9: "But you are a chosen race, a royal priesthood, a holy nation, God's own people, in order that you may proclaim the mighty acts of him who called you out of darkness into his marvelous light."[1]

*But why should I praise God when so much has gone wrong in my life?*

Padre Pio's assurance: "At the sight of all the help which Jesus offers me with such great liberality, I can't contain the transports of my gratitude. In the midst of the extreme desolation in which the Lord has placed me, I feel a sentiment of gratitude which rises up like a giant in my heart. But, as a grace, this is a thousand miles from my spirit, or rather admitting that it is a grace for me, I do not believe it is for my good, for I see very clearly that my soul is quite unworthy of God's light which enlightens every person who comes into this world."[2]

"My soul is full of gratitude to God for the many victories it obtains at every instant, and I cannot refrain from uttering endless hymns of blessing to this great and munificent God. Blessed be the Lord for this great goodness. Blessed be his great mercy. Eternal praise be to such a tender and loving compassion!"[3]

*Lord, don't let me focus on the negatives. Help me to always give you thanks and praise for the many blessings you give me every day. Amen.*

# *Guardian Angels*

Psalm 91:11: "For he will command his angels concerning you / to guard you in all your ways."[1]

*But I make so many mistakes, and I sin every day. Why would God bother to assign a holy angel to watch over me?*

Padre Pio's assurance: ". . . never forget your guardian angel who is always close to you, who never leaves you, no matter how badly you treat him. O unspeakable excellence of this good angel of ours! How many times, alas, have I made him weep when I refused to comply with his wishes which were also God's wishes. May this most faithful friend of ours save us from further unfaithfulness."[2]

"How consoling to know one is always under the protection of a heavenly spirit who never abandons us, not even when we are actually offending God. How delightful is this great truth to the one who believes. Who is to be feared, then, by the devout soul who is trying to love Jesus, when accompanied by such an illustrious warrior?"[3]

"May your good guardian angel break down and reduce to silence all the tempter's cunning suggestions."[4]

*Lord, enable my heart and soul to hear and obey the guidance of my holy guardian angel who always follows your will. Thank you. Amen.*

# *Jesus Our Guide*

Isaiah 58:11: "The LORD will guide you continually, / and satisfy your needs in parched places, / and make your bones strong; / and you shall be like a watered garden, / like a spring of water, / whose waters never fail."[1]

*But the path over which he leads me snakes through storms and deserts, swamps and wilderness.*

Padre Pio's assurance: "Pay little attention to the path on which the Lord places you. . . . But rather, keep your eyes always fixed on he who guides you, and on the heavenly homeland to which he wants to lead you. Why should you worry whether Jesus wants you to reach the homeland by way of the desert or through fields, when one way or the other you will reach blessed eternity just the same?

"Drive away all excessive worry which springs from the trials through which the good Lord wants to visit you, and if this is not possible, drive the thought away and live resigned to divine will in everything.

"I don't mean to disapprove of your praying that God might console you. . . . But . . . if he is not pleased to do so, be ready to say the fiat [so be it] with Jesus."[2]

*Heavenly Father, give me the grace to always say "fiat" with Jesus, to always follow wherever you lead, even if you lead me over rough paths. Amen.*

# Handmaid of the Lord

Luke 1:38: "Then Mary said, 'Here am I, the servant [handmaid] of the Lord; let it be with me according to your word.' "[1]

*But but how can I have the faith to always say "God's will be done"?*

Padre Pio's assurance: "Don't worry; abandon yourself to the divine heart of Jesus and leave all your cares to him. Always place yourself last among those who love the Lord, considering everybody to be better than you. . . . The more that graces and favors grow in your soul, the more you should humble yourself, always maintaining the humility of our heavenly Mother, who, the instant she became the Mother of God, declared herself to be the servant and handmaid of the same God. Both in happy and sad events, always humble yourself under the powerful hand of God, humbly and patiently accepting not only that which pleases your senses, but even more so, accepting all the tribulations he sends you in order to render you acceptable to him and always more worthy of the heavenly homeland."[2]

"May the most holy Virgin obtain for us love of the cross . . . and may she who was first to practice the Gospel in all its perfection before it was written, enable us and stimulate us to follow her example."[3]

*Lord, thank you for your Mother, my Mother. May she always guide me along the humble path that leads to you. Amen.*

# *Happiness*

Psalm 144:15: "Happy are the people to whom such blessings fall; / happy are the people whose God is the LORD."[1]

*But happiness so often eludes me. Where can I find it?*

Padre Pio's assurance: "When Mass was over, I remained with Jesus in thanksgiving. Oh how sweet was the colloquy with paradise that morning. It was such that, although I want to tell you all about it, I cannot. There were things which cannot be translated into human language without losing their deep and heavenly meaning. The heart of Jesus and my own were fused. No longer were two hearts beating, but only one. My own heart had disappeared, as a drop of water is lost in the ocean. Jesus was its paradise, its King. My joy was so intense and deep that I could bear no more, and tears of happiness poured down my cheeks.

". . . When paradise is poured into a heart, this afflicted, exiled, weak, and mortal heart cannot bear it without weeping."[2]

"How happy is the interior kingdom when [God's] holy love reigns within it. How blessed are the faculties of the soul when they obey so wise a King."[3]

*Lord, reign in my soul, not only so that happiness may dwell there, but also so that I will love and serve you all the days of my life. Amen.*

# Health of Body and Soul

3 John 2: "Beloved, I pray that all may go well with you and that you may be in good health, just as it is well with your soul."[1]

*But sin sickens my soul; how can my body have good health?*

Padre Pio's assurance: ". . . preservation of one's health must be practiced by every good and devout soul, because health cannot be bought; it is a gift from God. . . ."[2]

"If Providence has deprived us of our motive for neglecting spiritual things while we were busy improving our bodily life, God in his infinite wisdom has placed in our hands all the necessary means for the embellishment of our souls, even after we have disfigured them by sin. The soul's cooperation with divine grace is all that is required to enable it to develop, to reach such a degree of splendor and beauty as to attract, not so much the loving and astonished gaze of the angels, but the gaze of God himself. . . ."[3]

"May God be blessed forever, for he alone knows how to bring about these marvels [health] in a soul that always resisted him, a soul that was the receptacle of an infinite amount of filth. . . . Let sinners . . . hope in God."[4]

*Lord, thank you for your infinite mercy. Forgive me my many sins. Cleanse and heal my soul and — if you will — my body, too. Amen.*

# *Christ's Heart*

Matthew 11:29: ". . . learn from me; for I am gentle and humble in heart. . . ."[1]

*But how can I imitate Christ's gentleness and humility? I'm not God.*

Padre Pio's assurance: "You must hide yourself in this [Christ's] heart; you must pour out your desires in this heart; you must live in this heart the remaining days that providence will grant you; you must die in this heart when the Lord wishes.

"The soul who has chosen divine love cannot remain selfish in the heart of Jesus, but feels itself burn also with love for its brothers and sisters, which often causes the soul to suffer agonies.

"But how can all this take place? Given that the soul no longer lives its own life, but lives in Jesus who lives within the soul, it must feel, want, and live of the same sentiments and wishes of he who lives within it. And you know of the sentiments and desires, which animate the heart of this divine Master, for God and humanity."[2]

"The most afflicted souls are those chosen by the divine heart, and Jesus has chosen your soul to be the chosen one of his adorable heart."[3]

*Christ Jesus, hide my soul in your heart so that I may always imitate your gentleness and humility. Thank you. Amen.*

# *Your Heart*

Proverbs 23:26: "My child, give me your heart, / and let your eyes observe my ways."[1]

*But I'm afraid to give everything to God.*

Padre Pio's assurance: "Carry on tranquilly, for the divine mercy will not be lacking, and much less will it be lacking in your case if you show docility beneath the Lord's divine action. Don't be stingy with this heavenly physician. Don't keep him waiting any longer. To you, too, he is saying, 'Give me your heart,[2] so that I may pour my oil into it.' Let the invitation of such a tender Father not be wasted. Open the door of your heart to him with trustful abandonment. Don't hold up the precious stream of his oil as it is poured upon you, lest you have to go in search of this oil of his mercy at the hour of death[3] like the foolish virgins of the Gospel, for you will then find nobody willing to give it to you. Yes, during life always remain united with Jesus in the olive grove as he suffers his agony. By sharing thus, in the anointing of his grace and the comfort of his strength, you will find yourself after death among the same olive trees to share in the joy of his ascension and his glory."[4]

*Lord, I give you my heart. Fill it with your oil, even if doing so unites me with your suffering as well as with your glory. Amen.*

# *Heaven, the Right Port*

1 Peter 1:3-4: "By his [God's] great mercy he has given us a new birth into a living hope through the resurrection of Jesus Christ from the dead, and into an inheritance . . . kept in heaven for you. . . ."[1]

*But trials threaten to overwhelm and deprive me of that inheritance.*

Padre Pio's assurance: "Be at peace always in the arms of the Savior who loves you tenderly. . . .This holy love on which ours is founded, rooted, grown, and nourished will be eternally perfect and permanent."[2]

"Do your best to conform always and in everything to the will of God. This is the sure path to heaven."[3]

"This is the path [trials] by which Jesus leads strong souls. Here you will learn the better to recognize your true homeland and to look on this life as a brief pilgrimage."[4]

"The desire to be in eternal peace is good and holy, but you must moderate this with complete resignation to divine will."[5]

"Let us do good; let us adhere to the will of God. Let this be the star on which we rest our gaze throughout this navigation because in that way we cannot but reach the right port."[6]

*Lord, keep my gaze fixed on you. Hold me in your arms and guide me always in the way I should go. Amen.*

Padre Pio often heard confessions from morning until night, eager to help people reconcile with God. "God does not reject poor sinners, and he will not reject you" (*Letters, Volume III*).

# *Help Divine*

Hebrews 4:16: "Let us therefore approach the throne of grace with boldness, so that we may receive mercy and find grace to help in time of need."[1]

*But I have asked God to help me, and my troubles only increase.*

Padre Pio's assurance: "Try to believe that your present state [suffering] is a most singular grace from the divine Father; a grace which he grants you despite all your unworthiness."[2]

"Do not think that your present state is a punishment from heaven, because you would be wrong, but be certain that your present state is willed by God for the salvation of your soul."[3]

"After the abandonment and surrender of your entire self to Jesus, always remember that you are no longer yours, but that you belong to him. He will take care of sustaining and helping you. . . . Be tranquil and do not fear the roars of Satan because Jesus will always inspire you with great courage in order to weaken him."[4]

"May the grace of the divine Spirit assist you in the hour of trial and make you always triumph over everything!"[5]

*Lord, grant me the grace to always focus on you, rather than on my sufferings. In you I will find courage, perseverance, and peace. Amen.*

# *Holy Communion*

Matthew 5:48: "Be perfect, therefore, as your heavenly Father is perfect."[1]

*But how can I, a sinner, reach perfection, at least in this life?*

Padre Pio's assurance: "The Holy Eucharist is a great means through which to aspire to perfection. But we must receive it with the desire and intention of removing from the heart all that is displeasing to him with whom we wish to dwell."[2]

"As soon as you are before God in the Blessed Sacrament, devoutly genuflect. Once you have found your place, kneel down and render the tribute of your presence and devotion to Jesus in the Blessed Sacrament. Confide all your needs to him, along with those of others. Speak to him with filial abandonment, give free rein to your heart, and give him complete freedom to work in you as he thinks best."[3]

"Never neglect to satiate yourself with the food of the angels. The temptations you will receive from the enemy will be many, for he is not unaware of the benefit your soul receives from this food. But you must not be frightened. Jesus promises that he will not cease to assist you."[4]

*Lord, draw me as often as you will to Holy Communion. Through this Sacrament, through your presence within me, I can reach perfection. Amen.*

# *Holy Spirit*

Romans 8:27: "... the Spirit intercedes for the saints [us] according to the will of God."[1]

Hebrews 7:25: "... he always lives to make intercession for them."[2]

*But fear of having offended him beyond forgiveness haunts me.*

Padre Pio's assurance: "The fear which you have with regard to sins committed is illusory and a real torment brought about by the devil. Have you not confessed these sins? Of what then are you afraid? Once and for all ... open up your heart to a holy and unbounded trust in Jesus [and his Holy Spirit]. Believe that God is not the cruel taskmaster depicted for you by that perpetrator of iniquity, but the Lamb who takes away the sins of the world,[3] interceding for our salvation with sighs too deep for words."[4]

"Give yourself up to all his [the Holy Spirit's] transports and have no fear. He is so wise and gentle and discreet that he never brings about anything but good. How good this Holy Spirit, this Comforter, is to all, but how supremely good he is to those who seek him."[5]

"May the Holy Spirit fill you with his most holy gifts, sanctify you, guide you ... and comfort you in your innumerable troubles."[6]

*Lord, I offer myself to your wise and gentle Holy Spirit. Even in my troubles and sinfulness, I will trust in your mercy and love. Amen.*

# Holy Trinity

Matthew 28:19: ". . . make disciples of all nations, baptizing them in the name of the Father and of the Son and of the Holy Spirit. . . ."[1]

1 Corinthians 3:17: "Do you not know that you are God's temple and that God's Spirit dwells in you?"[2]

*But why would God choose to live inside me, such a weak person?*

Padre Pio's assurance: "As Saint Paul says, 'though he [Christ Jesus] was in the form of God,[3] and in him the whole fullness of deity dwells bodily,'[4] he did not disdain to lower himself to our level in order to raise us up to fullness of life in God.

"Of his own free will and to the fullest extent, this divine Word was pleased to abase himself to our level, by hiding his divine nature beneath the veil of human flesh."[5]

"Neither did he [Jesus] obey for the sake of reward, as he himself was God and equal in all things to the Father."[6]

". . . Do not let the enemy find the way to enter your soul and contaminate the temple of the Holy Spirit. . . . At our Baptism we became temples of the living God. . . ."[7]

*Holy Trinity, cleanse my soul and don't let the enemy contaminate it. Make me your holy temple. Amen.*

# *Hope*

1 Peter 1:21: "Through him [Christ] you have come to trust in God, who raised him from the dead and gave him glory, so that your faith and hope are set on God."[1]

*But the uncertainty of my future sometimes clouds all hope.*

Padre Pio's assurance: "A soul who trusts in the Lord and places all its hope in him has nothing to fear. The enemy of our salvation is always around us to snatch from our hearts the anchor that is to lead us to salvation, by which I mean trust in God our Father. Let us keep a firm hold on this anchor and not relinquish it for a single moment."[2]

"Hope in God and expect everything that is good from him. Don't dwell on what the enemy presents to you . . . stop thinking of it and turn to God. Bend your knee before him and with the greatest humility say this short prayer, 'Have mercy on me a poor weakling.' "[3]

"I am oppressed by the uncertainty of my future, but I cherish the lively hope of seeing my dreams fulfilled because the Lord cannot place thoughts and desires in a person's soul if he does not really intend to fulfill them, to gratify these longings which he alone has caused."[4]

*Lord, I place all my hope in you, trusting you to lead me every step of the way in fulfilling the dreams and desires you have planted in my soul. Amen.*

# *Humility*

1 Peter 5:5: "... clothe yourselves with humility in your dealings with one another, for 'God opposes the proud, but gives grace to the humble.' "[1]

*But my pride insists that I race ahead of God in order to avoid trials.*

Padre Pio's assurance: "... try more and more to hold firmly to humility and charity which are the main supports of the whole vast building and on which all the rest depends. . . . If the heart is always striving to practice these two virtues, it will meet with no difficulty in practicing the others."[2]

"When you are unable to take big steps on the paths along which the Lord leads you, be content with small steps and patiently wait until you have the legs to run, or better still, wings to fly. Be content with being a little honeybee in a hive for the present; a little bee that will quickly become a big bee, able to manufacture honey, because God speaks to those who are humble."[3]

"Humble yourself under the mighty hand of God,[4] accepting with submission and patience the tribulations he sends you, so that he can exalt you in due time,[5] by giving you his grace."[6]

*Lord, give me the grace to humble myself before you, to wait for your directions, and to bear my trials with patience. Thank you. Amen.*

# *Hurry at Christ's Every Invitation*

John 7:37-39: ". . . while Jesus was standing there, he cried out, 'Let anyone who is thirsty come to me, and let the one who believes in me drink. As the scripture has said, 'Out of the believer's heart shall flow rivers of living water.' Now he said this about the Spirit. . . ."[1]

*But so many times I have run away from God; why would he offer me his graces, his Spirit now?*

Padre Pio's assurance: "It rends my heart to see so many poor blind souls who flee more quickly than they would from fire when they hear the divine Master's most tender invitation: 'Let anyone who is thirsty come to me, and let the one who believes in me drink.'[2]

"Jesus invites you to go and quench your thirst with this ever-living water [the Holy Spirit]. He knows well your need to drink your fill of this new water, which he keeps in readiness for those who really thirst, so that they may not perish in the flames which are devouring them."[3]

"May it please the Lord, the source of all life, not to deny you this sweet and precious water which in his super-abundant love he has promised to those who thirst for it."[4]

*Lord, in spite of my failure to accept your invitation in the past, enable me to accept it now — and forever. Amen.*

# Impatience

Hebrews 6:15: "And thus Abraham, having patiently endured, obtained the promise."[1]

*But what should I do when impatience takes over?*

Padre Pio's assurance: "Let your entire life be spent in resignation, prayer, work, humility, and rendering thanks to the good God. If you happen to notice a feeling of impatience arising, immediately pray. Consider that we are always in the presence of God, to whom we have to give account for our every action, both good and bad. . . . I want the thought of the suffering and humiliation of Jesus to be the usual subject of your meditation. If you practice this, in a short time you will experience its salutary fruits. Such meditation will act as a shield to defend you from impatience when the most sweet Jesus sends you suffering, places you in a state of desolation, or wishes to make you a subject of contradiction."[2]

"Be at peace about everything, and don't worry. You live for the sole purpose of doing the will of this most sweet lover of ours. When you feel distressed, wait patiently for this tender spouse, and you will see that he will not let you suffer at length without being consoled."[3]

*Lord, thank you that you will never let me suffer long without consoling me. Plant patience in my soul, so that I always wait for you to lead. Amen.*

# *Imperfections*

James 1:3-4: ". . . and let endurance have its full effect, so that you may be mature and complete [perfect], lacking in nothing."[1]

*But I have too many imperfections to ever attain perfection.*

Padre Pio's assurance: "Be patient and don't become discouraged if you see yourself still full of imperfections."[2] ". . . There is nothing that nourishes our defects like restlessness, and the haste to drive them away."[3]

"Now you should take courage, take a breath, and consider the dangers met [in the past] from which the vigilant hand of the Lord freed you, despite your every unworthiness. . . . Be suspicious of all those desires which cannot be attained. These are all those desires for some Christian perfection which can be imagined and admired, but not practiced, and about which many speak without putting it into practice."[4]

"You cannot mortify the flesh entirely as there is always some rebellion. Our attention will often be interrupted by distractions, but should we perhaps worry . . . and become afflicted by all this? Never."[5]

"We must resign ourselves to bearing our imperfections in order to arrive at perfection."[6]

*Lord, give me patience with which to bear my imperfections, and help me to gradually overcome them, for love of you. Amen.*

# Like a Child in a Mother's Arms

Isaiah 66:13: "As a mother comforts her child, / so I will comfort you. . . ."[1]

*But I left childhood long ago, and so now I must face fear alone.*

Padre Pio's assurance: "If we were left to ourselves, we should always be falling and never remain on our feet. Humble yourself, then, at the delightful thought that you are in the divine arms of Jesus, the best of fathers, like a little infant in its mother's arms, and sleep peacefully with the certainty that you are being guided toward the destination which will be to your greatest advantage. How can we be afraid to remain in such loving arms when our entire being is consecrated to God?"[2]

"To be afraid of being lost while you are in the arms of divine goodness is stranger than fear on the part of a child in its mother's arms."[3]

"So do not become too uneasy in the hour of trial, but try to bear everything with love. Jesus will be favorable towards you and will grant you the grace to lead a totally heavenly life, and nothing will be able to separate you from his love."[4]

". . . Live tranquilly because Jesus is with you always, and you rest sweetly on his heart like a child in the arms of its mother."[5]

*Heavenly Father, hold me in your arms and assure me that, in your embrace, all will be well. Amen.*

In his desire to encourage the faithful, Padre Pio said, "Jesus will always sustain you in everything" (*Letters, Volume III*).

# *In a World Lost By God*

1 John 2:15-17: ". . . all that is in the world — the desire of the flesh, the desire of the eyes, the pride in riches — comes not from the Father but from the world. And the world and its desire are passing away, but those who do the will of God live forever."[1]

*But I live in this world; how do I separate myself from it?*

Padre Pio's assurance: "May Jesus always be your greatness and the world your contempt. The world believes it has already lost you; it no longer considers you to belong to it. We must always be careful not to let it gain us once again, because allowing yourself to be won over by this wretched world, which God has lost and will lose in eternity, would mean you would be totally lost. The world will . . . look upon you with honor when it sees you diligently preserving the rules of piety and devotion, a piety and devotion that is wise, earnest, strong, noble, and totally sweet.

"Always be resigned in all the misfortunes of this life. You know well that God reserves his children for a future life and that for the present he usually grants nothing to his chosen ones except the honor of tolerating a great deal and carrying their cross after him."[2]

*Lord, by your grace I will not allow the world to win me back to its corrupt self. Help me to accept with joy the cross you offer me. Amen.*

# *Infant Jesus*

Luke 2:7: "And she gave birth to her firstborn son and wrapped him in bands of cloth, and laid him in a manger, because there was no place for them in the inn."[1]

*But why focus on the sufferings that Mary, Joseph, and Jesus endured?*

Padre Pio's assurance: "Wouldn't you have chosen to be in that dark stable filled with the cries of the little child, rather than beside yourself with joy, with the shepherds at this sweet heavenly melody and the beauty of this admirable splendor? Yes. . . .

"You are nowhere but close to the infant Jesus, trembling with cold in the stable of Bethlehem. . . . You are on Calvary with the Marys, where you see nothing but death, nails, thorns, powerlessness, extraordinary darkness, abandonment, and dereliction. Therefore, I beg you to love the crib of the child of Bethlehem; love the Calvary of the God crucified amidst the darkness; stay close to him and know that Jesus is in the midst of your hearts more than you could believe or imagine."[2]

"May the heavenly child always be at the center of your heart. May he sustain it, enlighten it, inspire it, and transform it to his eternal charity."[3]

*Infant Jesus, dwell in my heart; keep me close to you in your suffering, so that I can embrace my own and help others to bear theirs. Amen.*

# Intention to Please God

1 Thessalonians 4:1: "Finally, brothers and sisters, we ask and urge you in the Lord Jesus that, as you learned from us how you ought to live and to please God (as, in fact, you are doing), you should do so more and more."[1]

*But how can I please God? Even when I pray, many things interrupt and distract me.*

Padre Pio's assurance: "Don't worry if you feel cold when you meditate and pray . . . and if you see yourself still surrounded by weakness, because given that this takes place against your every will, there is no fault, and is nothing but a source of merit for you.

"These are the trials of chosen souls whom God wants to put to the test when he sees they have the necessary strength to sustain the battle. . . .

"Continue to practice meditation and all the other devout practices, always renewing your upright intentions, and do not be at all upset if you are unable to do all this with that perfection you would desire.

"Be certain of God's love for you and of his complete and total pardon for your errors. Believe this firmly and do not wrong divine goodness by doubting this."[2]

*Lord, thank you for your patience, love, and mercy. Give me patience with myself, and don't ever let me give up the "battle." Amen.*

# *Intercession*

1 Timothy 2:1: "First of all, then, I urge that supplications, prayers, intercessions, and thanksgivings be made for everyone. . . ."[1]

*But my prayers can't possibly make a difference in the lives of others.*

Padre Pio's assurance: "Recommend me always to the Lord . . . so that he might allow me to accomplish his lovable will always. . . .

"Pray a great deal and do not waste time, because the catastrophe is imminent, and if he [God] doesn't intervene soon, it is inevitable.

"I beg you to make the novena to the Virgin in order to obtain those said graces. Help me in this most lofty mission, and we will share the reward also."[2]

"You ask me if it is a useful thing to apply the sacrifice of the Mass for the living. It is extremely useful and holy to apply this sacrifice while one is a pilgrim on this earth, and it will help us to live a holy life, and extinguish the debts contracted with divine justice, and render the most sweet Lord more benevolent toward us."[3]

"Fear nothing, however. Live peacefully and pray that the Lord may enlighten you along with he who has the task of directing you."[4]

*Inspire me to pray always and to intercede for others in their needs, including those in power over us. Thanks for always listening, Lord. Amen.*

# Jesus, Most Compassionate and Tender

James 5:11: "You have heard of the endurance of Job, and you have seen the purpose of the Lord, how the Lord is compassionate and merciful."[1]

*But weakness and fatigue threaten to keep me from enduring like Job.*

Padre Pio's assurance: "I feel very weak, it is true, but I am not afraid on this account, for will Jesus not see my anguish and the weight that oppresses me? He has told us by the mouth of the royal prophet that, 'As a father has compassion for his children, so the Lord has compassion for those who fear him. For he knows how we were made; he remembers that we are dust.'[2] The Lord then consoles me and causes me to 'boast all the more gladly of my weaknesses.' "[3]

"I am glad to have to manifest all the gratuitous favors which Jesus has bestowed on my soul.

"I fully recognize that there is nothing in me capable of attracting the gaze of this most tender Jesus of ours. His goodness alone has filled my soul with many good things. . . . He follows me everywhere, revives my life poisoned by sin, disperses the dense clouds which had enveloped my soul after I had sinned."[4]

*Lord, thank you that your compassionate and tender presence will always empower me to endure, no matter what enters my life. Amen.*

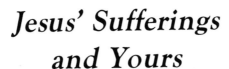

# Jesus' Sufferings and Yours

1 Peter 4:12-13: "Beloved, do not be surprised at the fiery ordeal that is taking place among you to test you. . . . But rejoice insofar as you are sharing Christ's sufferings, so that you may also be glad and shout for joy when his glory is revealed."[1]

*But how can I find joy and gladness in suffering?*

Padre Pio's assurance: "I am suffering very much, but thanks to our good Jesus I still feel a little strength, and when aided by Jesus, what [good] is the creature not capable of doing? . . . I am happy to suffer with Jesus. In contemplating the cross on his shoulders, I feel more and more fortified, and I exult with holy joy."[2]

"So let us not weep. . . . Jesus chooses souls, and despite my unworthiness, he has chosen mine also to help him in the tremendous task of men's salvation.

"This is the whole reason why I desire to suffer. . . . In this consists all my joy. Unfortunately, I am in need of courage, but Jesus will not refuse anything. I can testify to this from long experience, so we should not stop asking him for what we need."[3]

*Dear Lord, use me for the salvation of others — as well as my own. Amen.*

# *Joyfulness*

John 16:22: "So you have pain now; but I will see you again, and your hearts will rejoice, and no one will take your joy from you."[1]

*But can't I now have some of that joy?*

Padre Pio's assurance: "Joy is born of happiness at possessing what we love. Now, from the moment at which the soul knows God, it is naturally led to love him. If the soul follows this natural impulse which is caused by the Holy Spirit, it is already loving the supreme good. This fortunate soul already possesses the beautiful virtue of love. . . . When a person loves money, honors, and good health, unfortunately, he does not always possess what he loves, whereas he who loves God possesses him at once.

"Joy, then, is an offspring of love, but if this joy is to be true and perfect, it must be accompanied inseparably by the peace which pervades us when the good we possess is supreme and certain.

"Our divine Master assures us that 'no one will take your joy from you.'[2] What testimony could be more certain than this? Pondering all this, one cannot fail to experience great gladness. This is what leads people to face the most painful trials with a cheerful heart."[3]

*Lord, thank you for the joy that comes from loving you. Amen.*

# *Justification*

Romans 5:1-2: "Therefore, since we are justified by faith, we have peace with God through our Lord Jesus Christ, through whom we have obtained access to this grace in which we stand. . . ."[1]

*But how can faith justify me, cleanse me of sin, fill me with peace?*

Padre Pio's assurance: "Let us pray to the Father of all light to enable us to penetrate more and more deeply into the mystery of our justification, how wretched sinners like ourselves have been led to salvation. Our justification is such an enormous miracle that sacred scripture compares it to the resurrection of our divine Master.[2] . . . God revealed his power more fully in our justification than in creating heaven and earth from nothing. . . . In fact, since nonexistence is the lack of being, it has no power to resist God's will, while the sinner as a being, and a free being, is capable of resisting all God's wishes."[3]

"Oh, if we could only perceive for a single instant that which still amazes the heavenly spirits, namely, the state to which God's grace has raised us, to be nothing less than his own children, destined to reign with his Son for all eternity."[4]

*Lord, thank you for the faith and love with which you — in spite of my sinfulness — justify and save me. Don't ever let me resist you again. Amen.*

# Kiss of the Divine Mouth

Song of Solomon 1:2: "Let him kiss me with the kisses of his mouth!"[1]

*But how can I receive God's "kisses" when I don't deserve them?*

Padre Pio's assurance: "May you be consoled by the sweet thought of your love for Jesus and of being loved by him much more in return. Let us ask him for the grace to love him and to see him loved more and more. Let us ask him this with the spouse of the holy Song: 'Let him kiss me with the kisses of his mouth! For your love is better than wine'[2] . . . Yes, let us ardently desire this kiss of the divine mouth, and still more, let us show our gratitude for it."[3]

"We must continually implore two things from our most tender Lord: that he increase within us love and fear, for this will make us fly in the ways of the Lord. It will make us careful where we set foot, make us see the things of the world for what they are, and lead us to beware of all negligence. Then when love and fear have kissed, it is no longer in our power to give our affection to the things of this world. We no longer experience strife or envy. Our only desire on this earth is to delight the loved one, and we feel ourselves dying of the desire to be loved by him."[4]

*Please increase love and holy fear in me, so that I may delight and love you as you will. Always "kiss" me with the peace of your presence. Amen.*

# *Knock*

Luke 11:9: "So I say to you, ask, and it will be given you; search, and you will find; knock, and the door will be opened for you."[1]

*But I do knock on God's door, and sometimes it seems as if no one answers.*

Padre Pio's assurance: "Let us keep our thoughts continually fixed on heaven, our true homeland of which this earth is merely an image. Let us be cheerful and calm in all circumstances, whether happy or sad, as is fitting . . . to a soul that has received special training at the school of suffering.

"May the motives of faith and the comfort of Christian hope offer you continual support in all this. If you act in this way, the heavenly Father will alleviate your trial with the balm of his goodness and mercy. The holy and beneficent angel of faith counsels and urges us to have recourse by insistent, humble prayer to this goodness and mercy of the heavenly Father, in the firm hope that we shall be heard. In this we are basing our trust on the promise made to us by the divine Master: 'Ask, and it will be given you; search, and you will find; knock, and the door will be opened for you. . . .' "[2]

". . . Let us pray and continue to pray because intense and fervent prayer pierces the heavens and is backed up by a divine guarantee."[3]

*Lord, even when it seems as if you don't hear or care about me, keep me knocking — with faith in your love for me — at the door of your heart. Amen.*

Padre Pio kept his eyes, heart, and soul focused on Jesus, to whom he gave the credit for any good he did. "Nothing is due to me. I am an instrument in divine hands; an instrument which only succeeds in serving some purpose when it is handled by the divine Craftsman" (*Letters, Volume III*).

# *Lest You Dash Your Foot*

Psalm 91:12: "On their hands they [angels] will bear you up, / so that you will not dash your foot against a stone."[1]

*But will my own angel help me throughout life, no matter what?*

Padre Pio's assurance: "May your good guardian angel always watch over you; may he be your guide on the bitter paths of life. May he always keep you in the grace of Jesus and sustain you with his hands so that you may not stumble on a stone.

"Have great devotion to this good angel. How consoling it is to know that near us is a spirit who, from the cradle to the tomb, does not leave us even for an instant, not even when we dare to sin. And this heavenly spirit guides and protects us like a friend, a brother.

"It is consoling to know that this angel prays without ceasing for us; he offers to God all our good actions, thoughts, desires, if they are pure.

"For pity's sake, don't forget this invisible companion, always present, always ready to listen to us, and even more ready to console us."[2]

"May your good angel remain watchful by your side, may he protect you and support you with his hands lest you dash your foot against a stone."[3]

*Lord, thank you for the holy angel you assigned to me. Remind me to always show him gratitude and love — and to rely on him for help. Amen.*

# *Life*

Galatians 2:19-20: "I have been crucified with Christ; and it is no longer I who live, but it is Christ who lives in me."[1]

*But I need assurance that Christ truly does live and work within me, especially since I continue to stumble and blunder my way through life.*

Padre Pio's assurance: "In the hour of trial, don't tire yourself in trying to find God. He is within you even then, in a most intimate manner. He is with you in your groanings and searching, just like a mother who urges her little child to seek her while she is behind him, and it is precisely her hands that encourage him to reach her."[2]

"At certain moments I am led to exclaim with the Apostle, although unfortunately not with the same perfection, 'It is no longer I who live, but it is Christ who lives in me.' "[3]

"Only pray that the little bit of life I have left may be spent for his glory and that I may make use of this time in such a way as to spread the light."[4]

"Let us consider that the divine bridegroom, not satisfied with the immense reward he has reserved [for us] in the next life in return for our love, intends to let us taste it even in this life."[5]

*Lord, I don't deserve that "taste" of heaven in this life, but I need it, especially when life threatens to squash me and I see only darkness ahead. Amen.*

# *Little Things*

Lk 16:10: "Whoever is faithful in a very little is faithful also in much. . . ."[1]

*But I'm tired of dealing with the little, insignificant duties of my life.*

Padre Pio's assurance: "Beware of complaining of being miserable and unhappy, because besides the fact that many expressions are unseemly for a servant of God, they also arise from an excessively dejected soul, and are nothing but impatience and resentment. Make a particular effort to practice sweetness and submission to the will of God, not only in extraordinary matters, but even in the little things that occur daily. Make these acts with a tranquil and joyful spirit. And if you should fail in this, humble yourself, make a new proposition, get up, and continue on your way.

". . . It is not necessary to philosophize except on one's improvements and progress in daily events, leaving the result of your desires to God's providence. Abandon yourself in his paternal arms like a child who, in order to grow, eats what her father prepares every day. . . ."[2]

"As you go about your daily business, examine yourself to see . . . if you always hold onto the Lord with one hand. . . . Calm your soul and let it rest again."[3]

*Lord, forgive my complaints about the little things in my life that seem so insignificant to me, but not to you. Take my hand and keep me faithful. Amen.*

# Lord Jesus, Lover of Your Soul

Psalm 33:22: "Let your steadfast love, O LORD, be upon us, / even as we hope in you."[1]

*But how can God love me when I so often offend him?*

Padre Pio's assurance: "My heart has found at last a lover so attached to me that I am incapable of hurting him anymore. You already know this lover. He is one who is never angry with those who offend him. My heart keeps within itself an infinite number of his mercies."[2]

"But observe the goodness of this divine lover who does not rebuff the soul, but draws it towards him by loving gestures."[3]

"The [Christ] child is the affectionate brother, the most loving spouse of our souls. . . ."[4]

"The divine bridegroom continues to reveal to the soul most important truths in a completely new way. The soul, however, does not perceive this divine lover who is manifesting himself. There is a mere awareness that he is there, close at hand, and the soul can have no doubts on this point. It finds itself in an atmosphere of such dazzling light; it experiences such wonderful effects of this union with the bridegroom. . . ."[5]

*Lord, I don't know why you love me, but don't ever stop. Amen.*

# *Love of God*

Matthew 22:37: "He said to him, 'You shall love the Lord your God with all your heart, and with all your soul, and with all your mind.' "[1]

*But I worry that I don't love him as I should.*

Padre Pio's assurance: "You are afraid . . . that you do not love God at all. Well, I urge you to be at peace on this point. Do you not feel this love in your own heart? What is that ardent desire you feel in your soul? Who placed in your heart this yearning to love the Lord? Do you think that holy desires can be inspired by anyone but God?

"Console yourself and be quite sure that God is not found where there is no desire for his love. Now, if the soul longs for nothing else than to love its God, which is your case, then don't worry. . . ."[2]

"I understand very well that nobody can worthily love God, but when a person does all he can and trusts in the divine mercy, why should Jesus reject one who is seeking him like this? . . . Well, then, if you have given and consecrated everything you have to God, why are you afraid?"[3]

"Be quite at peace as regards the existence of divine love in your heart. Cast aside all that futile anxiety and have no fear."[4]

*Lord, I long to love you more each day. Take my heart and fill it with your divine love so that love overflows to you — always. Amen.*

# Love of Neighbor

Luke 10:27: "He answered, 'You shall love the Lord your God . . . and your neighbor as yourself.' "[1]

*But how can I love my neighbor when I don't always love myself?*

Padre Pio's assurance: "As regards the virtues to be practiced in dealing with others, the first is kindliness. . . . [This is] a virtue which leads us to help others. . . . By this virtue the pious soul, by showing agreeable, courteous, and polite manners with no trace of uncouthness, draws others to imitate him in the devout life."[2]

". . . Add to [this virtue] the virtue of faithfulness, by which the devout soul gains the confidence of others and all become aware that his behavior is straightforward and free from duplicity."[3]

"Work without tiring among the children of men in order to render them all worthy children of God. Do not fear the anger of Satan who fumes on seeing you working for the cause of God. He is powerless against those who abandon themselves to God. Jesus and [Saint Francis of Assisi] will not fail to assist you."[4]

*Lord, teach me to love myself, so that I can also love others. Make me faithful, kind, courteous, polite, and straightforward, so that, by my example, I draw others to you. Amen.*

# Mary Magdalene and You

Luke 7:47-48, 50: " 'Therefore, I tell you, her sins, which were many, have been forgiven; hence she has shown great love. But the one to whom little is forgiven, loves little.' Then he said to her, 'Your sins are forgiven. . . . Your faith has saved you; go in peace.' "[1]

*But how can I believe God forgives me, and how can I "go in peace"? It was easy for Mary Magdalene to have faith; she saw Jesus face to face.*

Padre Pio's assurance: "Oh, if [you] were to imitate Mary Magdalene . . . and were to go through this same experience [of repentance], what abundant fruits of holiness would be yours. You would soon understand this secret, and by this means would soon be able . . . to change [God's] justice into loving mercy and obtain everything you need, forgiveness of your sins, grace, holiness, eternal salvation, and the power to overcome yourself and all your enemies."[2]

"Take heart, even when you feel oppressed by the number and atrocity of your offenses. Come to the feet of Jesus, who is fighting and enduring agony for us in the garden. . . . Ask for God's mercy, forgiveness, and help to walk all the time in his sight. Do this and have no doubt. . . ."[3]

*Lord, I come to your feet, begging for mercy and forgiveness of my sins. Help me to always walk in your sight, my hand in yours. Amen.*

# Mary Most Holy

Revelation 12:5: "And she gave birth to a son, a male child, who is to rule all the nations with a rod of iron."[1]

*But what does she, Mary Most Holy, have to do with me?*

Padre Pio's assurance: "When I think of the innumerable benefits received from this dear Mother, I am ashamed of myself, for I have never sufficiently appreciated her heart and her hand which have bestowed these benefits upon me with so much love. What troubles me most is that I have repaid the affectionate care of this Mother of ours by offending her.

"How often have I confided to this Mother the painful anxieties that troubled my heart. And how often has she consoled me. But in what did my gratitude consist? In my greatest sufferings, it seems to me that I no longer have a mother on this earth, but a very compassionate one in heaven. But many times, when my heart was at peace, I have forgotten all this almost entirely. I have even forgotten my duty of gratitude towards this blessed heavenly Mother."[2]

"But I am greatly indebted to our Mother Mary for driving away temptations of the enemy. Will you, too, thank this good Mother. . . ?"[3]

*Lord, thank you for Mary Most Holy. Please offer her my gratitude for the help she constantly gives me. Teach me to love her as you do. Amen.*

# Maxim of Padre Pio

Romans 8:28: "We know that all things work together for good for those who love God, who are called according to his purpose."[1]

*But does God make even sin and wickness "work together for good"?*

Padre Pio's assurance: "And in truth, given that the Lord can and is able to obtain good even from evil, for whom will he do this, if not for those who have given themselves to him without reservation?"[2]

"Consider the work of this great mercy: It converts our sins into good. . . . Tell me, therefore, what will he not do with our afflictions, with the troubles and persecutions which upset us? Therefore, if you ever happen to suffer for your afflictions, whatever they are, be certain that, if you love God with all your heart, everything will be converted to good. Even if at that moment you cannot understand where this good could come from, be more than ever sure that it will come, without a doubt.

"Therefore, don't be discouraged when you fall. . . . Your becoming discouraged and disheartened after the fall is the work of the enemy. . . . You will not do this, therefore, because the grace of God is always vigilant in coming to your aid."[3]

*Lord, help me to trust that — even when darkness surrounds me — you are working it all out for my good. Thank you. Amen.*

# *Meditation*

Psalm 19:14: "Let the words of my mouth and the meditation of my heart / be acceptable to you, / O LORD, my rock and my redeemer."[1]

*But I don't even know how to begin to meditate.*

Padre Pio's assurance: "Mental prayer or meditation is practiced as follows: First and foremost, prepare the subject of your meditation. There is not always a need to use a book in order to prepare this, as every truth of our religion can and must be a subject of meditation for the Christian soul."[2]

"Once the material for meditation has been prepared, place yourself in the presence of God, humbling yourself profoundly at the thought of who you are and to whom you are presenting yourself. Ask God for the grace of performing well the mental prayer you are about to practice, in order that you may obtain the fruit that God wants from it.

"Once you have done all this, offer your meditation and prayers. Along with your entire self — besides all those people who are dear to you — offer everything to God along with the merits of Jesus and of his Mother."[3]

"I give heartfelt thanks to the Lord for you because he makes you persevere in holy meditation."[4]

*Lord, help me to meditate each day on your life, on the truths of our Christian faith; and grant me the fruit of those mental prayers. Thank you. Amen.*

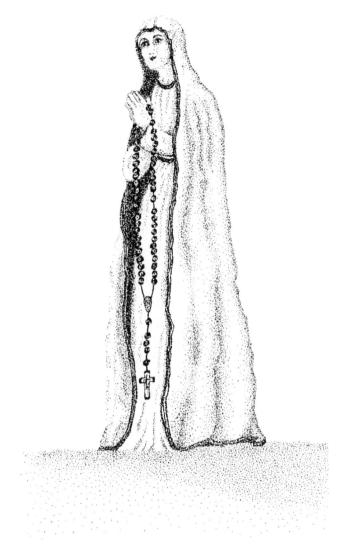

Padre Pio loved the Mother of God and wanted everyone to receive
God's graces through her intercession. "I wish I had a voice strong
enough to invite the sinners of the whole world to love Our Lady"
(*Letters, Volume I*).

# Mercy

1 Timothy 1:15-16: ". . . Christ Jesus came into the world to save sinners — of whom I am the foremost. But for that very reason I received mercy. . . ."[1]

*But I still fear that God won't want to show mercy to me.*

Padre Pio's assurance: "Your every fear is useless and lying; it is imaginary. Live tranquilly in the presence of God, who has loved you for a long time now. . . . Your miseries and weaknesses should not frighten you, because God has seen more serious ones within you and did not reject you for this, due to his mercy. So even less can he reject you now that you work untiringly for your perfection. God does not reject sinners, but rather grants them his grace, erecting the throne of his glory on their vileness.

"And you who were so miserable have experienced this heavenly goodness. Why do you fear then? . . . in the spiritual life it is necessary to walk in good faith, without uneasiness, discouragement, or sadness."[2]

". . . After being diligent and having done what you can, you can do no more for God except to ask him for his love, as he desires nothing more from you than this."[3]

*Lord, thank you for your mercy which reaches down to even a sinner like me. Love me and help me to always love you in return. Amen.*

# *Misery*

Job 11:13, 16: "If you direct your heart rightly, you will stretch out your hands toward him [God]. . . . You will forget your misery; you will remember it as waters that have passed away."[1]

*But misery drags me down, presses on my heart and soul. I feel powerless, and I can't imagine how I will ever forget this misery.*

Padre Pio's assurance: "You imagine that your powerlessness damages you, and it seems to you that this powerlessness prevents you from withdrawing into yourself and from moving closer to God. . . . You suppose wrongly. God has placed you in that state [misery] for his glory and your greater benefit. He wants your miseries to be the throne of his mercy, and your powerlessness, the seat of his omnipotence. Tell me, where did God put Samson's strength? Wasn't it in his hair, his weakest part?[2]

"Jesus is on your breast; he is within your heart. Isn't this enough to make you fight valiantly always? Isn't he the beginning and the end of all we could desire? One thing alone is necessary: to be close to him, and you are. . . . You need do no more than what you are already doing; love this divine goodness and abandon yourself into his arms and heart."[3]

*Lord, I abandon myself into your arms and heart; keep me always close to you. Amen.*

# My Guardian Dear

Matthew 18:10: "Take care that you do not despise one of these little ones; for, I tell you, in heaven their angels continually see the face of my Father in heaven."[1]

*But I'm no longer a child. Does an angel still guard me?*

Padre Pio's assurance: "Well, then, let me tell you that he [your guardian angel] is still powerful against Satan and his satellites. His [your angel's] love has not lessened [now that you are an adult], and he can never fail to defend you. . . . The fact that we have close to us an angelic spirit who never leaves us for an instant . . . must really fill us with consolation, especially in our more dreary moments.

"When it seems to you that you are alone and abandoned, don't complain that you are without a friend to whom you can open your heart and confide your woes. For goodness sake, don't forget this invisible companion who is always there to listen to you, always ready to console you.

"If all people could only understand and appreciate the great gift which God in his exceeding love has given us by appointing this heavenly spirit to guide us."[2]

*Lord, thank you for the consolation, companionship, and protection you provide me through my guardian angel. Help me to love him as you will. Amen.*

# *Our Blessed Mother Mary*

Luke 1:48-49: "For he has looked with favor on the lowliness of his servant [Mary]. Surely, from now on all generations will call me blessed; for the Mighty One has done great things for me, and holy is his name."[1]

*But can I follow Mary and, thereby, grow closer to her and her Son?*

Padre Pio's assurance: "Make every effort, like many elect souls, to follow invariably this Blessed Mother, to walk close to her since there is no other path leading to life except the path followed by our Mother. Let us not refuse to take this path, we who want to reach our journey's end. Let us invariably unite with this dear Mother. With her, close to Jesus. . . ."[2]

"My only regret is that I have no adequate means by which to thank the Blessed Virgin Mary, through whose intercession I have received so much strength from the Lord to bear with sincere resignation the many humiliations to which I am subjected day after day."[3]

"May Mary be the star which shines on your path, and may she show you the safe way to reach the heavenly Father."[4]

"May Jesus and the most holy Virgin make us worthy of eternal glory. With this faith and aspiration, I desire every blessing from heaven for you."[5]

*Lord, help me to always follow your Blessed Mother, and, in doing so, to follow you. Amen.*

# *Paradise*

Luke 23:42-43: "Then he said, 'Jesus, remember me when you come into your kingdom.' He replied, 'Truly I tell you, today you will be with me in Paradise.' "[1]

*But sometimes in my struggles I wonder if I'll ever get to paradise.*

Padre Pio's assurance: "How many tears and groans I send up to heaven in order to be set free [from my struggles]. But no matter, I will never tire of praying to Jesus. It is true that my prayers deserve punishment rather than reward, for I have offended Jesus only too often by my innumerable sins; but in the end he will be moved to pity for me and will either take me out of the world and call me to himself, or else he will set me free."[2]

"Again at night when I close my eyes, the veil is lifted and I see paradise open up before me; and gladdened by this vision, I sleep with a smile of sweet beatitude on my lips and perfectly tranquil countenance, waiting for the little companion [guardian angel] of my childhood to come to waken me, so that we may sing together the morning praises to the beloved of our hearts."[3]

*Lord, thank you for the promise of paradise for those who believe in you. If left to myself and my struggles, I would never reach heaven. But, "for God all things are possible."[4] Amen.*

# *Pardoned All*

Isaiah 55:7: "... let them return to the LORD, that he may have mercy on them, / and to our God, for he will abundantly pardon."[1]

*But I fear that even God can't pardon the many sins I've committed.*

Padre Pio's assurance: "The framework of your life should have no further reason to cause you to fear and be dejected in spirit. Jesus has pardoned everything; he has consumed everything with the fire of his holy love. The conviction to the contrary is not a thought that comes from God, but is a trick of the enemy who wants — if this were possible for him — to take you far from God and place you in the arms of discouragement. . . ."[2]

"Do not let the mass of your infidelities frighten you, for the Lord, who in sheer goodness has chosen you to be his beloved spouse, has pardoned and forgotten all. The trial to which God the Father has subjected you is not a punishment for your unfaithfulness. This is not so, I repeat, for he has forgotten everything. The trial has been sent to you in order to make you a more and more worthy bride of his beloved Son. This harsh trial is offered to you to enable you to collect more and more prizes and crowns to be presented to your spouse when you are united with him in heaven."[3]

*Lord, thank you for setting me free from my sins and guilt feelings. Amen.*

# Passion of Jesus

Philippians 3:10, 21: "I want to know Christ and the power of his resurrection and the sharing of his sufferings [passion]. . . . He will transform the body of our humiliation . . . the body of his glory. . . ."[1]

*But I don't want to suffer.*

Padre Pio's assurance: "May your way of life be totally heavenly; we are bound to this as Christians and also as children of the seraphic father, Saint Francis of Assisi. In imitation of this seraphic father, let us love Jesus in the passion. . . . Let us often meditate on the suffering of the God-Man, and then it will not be long before the great desire to suffer for love of Jesus is awakened in us. Love for the cross has always been the distinctive sign of chosen souls. . . . And our seraphic father understood well that without love for the cross, one cannot gain much profit in the ways of Christian perfection. Therefore, he continually carried — sculpted in his soul — the passion, death, and mortal life of the Son of God made Man. The fruits of such meditation was the generating in his heart of the love for suffering without limit. Often enraptured in loving ecstasy, he would exclaim [that the thought of heaven turned all his suffering into delight]."[2]

*Lord, whatever trials you send my way, please help me to bear them for love of you, keeping in view your promise of the joys of heaven. Amen.*

# *Paths*

Psalm 23:3: ". . . He leads me in right paths for his name's sake."[1]

*But how do I know if the path I'm following is that "right" path?*

Padre Pio's assurance: "Have no fear as regards your spirit because it is absolutely not true that you have taken the wrong path. The path you tread is the one that will lead you to heaven. And it is all the safer because Jesus himself takes you by the hand. Do not upset yourself at your spiritual aridity and desolation. On the contrary, console yourself in the tip of your spirit, and remember what our Lord said, 'Blessed are the poor in spirit, for theirs is the kingdom of heaven.' [2]

"What a joy it is to serve God in the desert without manna, water, or any other consolation except that of being under his guidance, and to suffer for him. May the most holy Virgin bring you her blessings.

"During this state of aridity and desolation of spirit, don't worry if you are unable to serve God as you would like. While you adapt to his wishes, you serve him according to his will, which is better than yours. What does it matter to us whether we belong to God in one way or another? In truth, as we seek nothing but him . . . we must be content with both paths."[3]

*Lord, lead me in the "right" path, and help me to find joy and peace in accepting it. Amen.*

# *Patience*

Luke 8:15: "But as for that in the good soil, these are the ones who, when they hear the word, hold it fast in an honest and good heart, and bear fruit with patient endurance."[1]

*But anxiety and longings tug at me until I want to race away from God.*

Padre Pio's assurance: "Now, to stand up to such harsh trials, the soul needs patience, a virtue which enables us to bear all adversity without giving in. Those who are striving for perfection must attribute great importance to this virtue unless they want their efforts to be completely wasted, for it is this virtue which maintains order in one's interior life."[2]

"I praise and bless God for his continual assistance in your regard and for the way he helps you to bear your trials without wavering. . . . 'By your endurance [patience] you will gain your souls,'[3] the divine Master tells us. It is therefore through patience that we will possess our souls, and to the extent to which it is perfect, will the possession of our souls be entire, perfect, and certain. Hence, the less it is mixed with longings and anxiety, the more perfect is our patience."[4]

*Lord, rid me of all anxiety and permeate my being with your patience, so that I never race ahead of you, but always follow you in peace. Amen.*

# *Peace*

John 14:27: "Peace I leave with you; my peace I give to you. I do not give to you as the world gives. Do not let your hearts be troubled, and do not let them be afraid."[1]

*But how do you avoid fear when your world threatens to collapse?*

Padre Pio's assurance: "The enemy of our salvation knows only too well that peace of heart is a sure sign of the divine assistance, and hence he lets slip no opportunity to make us lose this peace. We must therefore always be on our guard in this respect. Jesus will help us."[2]

"Strive to live in a holy and immutable peace. Jesus' yoke is easy and his burden light,[3] so we should not allow the enemy to creep into our hearts and rob us of this peace.

"Peace means order, harmony in our whole being; it means continual contentment springing from the knowledge of a good conscience; it is the holy joy of a heart in which God reigns."[4]

". . . [Pray] and wait for God to speak to you, because one day he will pronounce words of peace and consolation to you, and then you will know that your suffering served a good purpose and your patience was useful."[5]

*Lord, even when suffering tries to choke me with fear and anxiety, show me how to let go of it all and to allow your peace to envelop me. Amen.*

Though he suffered daily, Padre Pio experienced the joy of Christ dwelling within him. "Preserve a spirit of holy joyfulness," Pio said, "which, being modestly spread throughout your actions and words, brings consolation to others" (*Letters, Volume III*).

# *Perfection*

Hebrews 6:1: "Therefore let us go on toward perfection. . . ."[1]

*But no matter how hard I try, I still experience failures.*

Padre Pio's assurance: "You must not be discouraged or let yourself become dejected if your actions have not succeeded as perfectly as you intended. What do you expect? We are made of clay, and not every soil yields the fruits expected by the one who tills it. But let us always humble ourselves and acknowledge that we are nothing if we lack the divine assistance."[2]

"By the virtue of modesty the devout person governs all his exterior acts. . . . By self-restraint, the soul exercises restriction over all the senses: sight, touch, taste, smell, and hearing. By chastity, a virtue which ennobles our nature and makes it similar to that of the angels, we suppress our sensuality and detach it from forbidden pleasures.

"This is the magnificent picture of Christian perfection. Happy the one who possesses all these fine virtues, all of them fruits of the Holy Spirit, who dwells within that person. Such a soul has nothing to fear and will shine in the world as the sun in the heavens."[3]

*Lord, I now know the secret: I can't reach perfection, but you can do it through me. Do it, for the good of all people, and for your glory. Amen.*

# Power of Jesus' Name

Colossians 3:17: "And whatever you do, in word or deed, do everything in the name of the Lord Jesus. . . ."[1]

*But I don't understand.*

Padre Pio's assurance: ". . . [Jesus] was highly pleasing to the eternal Father, who exalted him and gave him the name — says the Apostle — 'that is above every name.'[2]

"It is by virtue of that name alone that we may hope to be saved, exactly as the Apostle declared before the Jews: 'There is no other name under heaven given among mortals by which we must be saved.'[3]

"The eternal Father decreed that all creatures should be subject to him, 'so that at the name of Jesus every knee should bend, in heaven and on earth and under the earth.'[4] This is what the Apostle tells us, and this is true. Jesus is adored in heaven. At this divine name, moved by gratitude and love, the blessed in heaven never cease to [praise him]."[5]

"As regards doing everything for God's glory, let us listen to the Apostle's teaching: 'And whatever you do, in word or deed, do everything in the name of the Lord Jesus. . . .' "[6]

*God, plant Jesus Christ's name deep within my heart, so that — in everything I do and say — I do it all in his name and for your glory. Amen.*

# Prayer

James 5:16: "The prayer of the righteous is powerful and effective."[1]

*But I'm certainly not righteous, so why would God answer my prayers?*

Padre Pio's assurance: "In the battles of life . . . the person who is bowed beneath the weight of tribulation, who is crushed by the sight of the wounds produced by his own failings and drags himself along face downward in the dust, who humbles himself, weeps, sighs, and prays, this person triumphs over God's justice and obliges God to show mercy. . . ."[2]

"Why should you get lost in vain fears which steal your time, upset your peace of mind, and make you almost diffident of God himself? For pity's sake, let us flee from these useless fears the moment they rise up in us. Let us never despair of the divine assistance. Would this not be an offense against the divine mercy? When these fears well up in you, remember the true Jacob who prayed in the garden;[3] remember that he discovered there the true ladder that connects earth with heaven; he showed us that humility, contrition, and prayer abolish the distance between man and God, bring God down to our level, and raise man up to God by causing the immense distance [between them] to disappear."[4]

*Lord, even though I am no saint, I'll keep praying, knowing that you will listen and answer me — in spite of me. Thank you. Amen.*

# *Precipice*

Ephesians 2:1, 8: "You were dead through the trespasses and sins in which you once lived. . . . By grace you have been saved through faith, and this is not your own doing; it is the gift of God. . . ."[1]

*But shouldn't I give myself some credit for my salvation?*

Padre Pio's assurance: ". . . I am overwhelmed with admiration at the goodness of our Lord, who has removed you from the path you were treading so heedlessly and which ended in a precipice. If Jesus had not enlightened you with his grace and drawn you to himself, you would have been like that foolish man who walked unwittingly all through the night along the riverbank, surrounded by deep darkness. . . . At a certain point the ground gave way beneath his feet, he fell in, and drowned.

"You, too, followed the road toward the precipice for a great part of the night, but Jesus' grace was so powerful that it was not confined to enlightening you and warning you of the real danger. . . . He drew you to himself by the power of love without encroaching on your own free will.

"You felt this loving power, and you could only yield to it. . . . He is always close to you; he rules and protects and sustains you. . . ."[2]

*Lord, help me to always give you all the credit for any good that I do. And don't ever leave me because without you I can only sin. Amen.*

# *Presence of God*

Psalm 16:11: "You show me the path of life. / In your presence there is fullness of joy. . . ."[1]

*But how can I experience God's presence and that fullness of joy?*

Padre Pio's assurance: "Often place yourself in the presence of God, and offer him all your actions and suffering."[2]

"Take care, moreover, not to lose the presence of God by any action whatsoever. Never undertake any action without first raising your mind to God and directing to him, with a pure intention, the action you are about to perform. You should do likewise at the end of every action."[3]

"Never let your mind become so absorbed in your work or in other matters as to make you lose the presence of God."[4]

"Place yourself in the presence of God during prayer in order to speak to him and to hear his voice through interior illumination. . . . It is a grace for us to speak to such a great Lord who, when he replies, spreads balms and precious ointments on us which render great sweetness to the soul."[5]

"Let the delightful thought console you that you are always in the presence of Jesus. . . ."[6]

*Lord, thank you that, even when I don't feel your presence, you are there. Keep me in your presence, on the "path of life," and filled with joy. Amen.*

# *Trusting in Self/Presumption*

Philippians 4:13: "I can do all things through him who strengthens me."[1]

*But don't I need to rely on my own strength too?*

Padre Pio's assurance: "A soul who felt its weakness and had recourse to God for help has never fallen. On the contrary, the soul is only defeated and overcome when, trusting in what it believes to be its abundant strength, thinks it can always sustain and bear temptations. Thus, it happens that the poor thing, out of presumption, believing it was touching the heavens, suddenly finds itself falling right to the doors of hell.

"Trust, therefore, and take heart. Don't let Satan's prolonged war frighten you; don't lose heart at the weakness you feel, because the soul that fears does not trust [itself], but stays awake and prays because of its weakness, and thus it becomes strong. But on the contrary, as unfailingly happens to those who trust in themselves, as if they were a god, they don't have to wait long before experiencing their miseries and weakness.

"Do not fear, but rather have greater confidence in divine mercy. Humble yourself before our merciful God and thank him for all the favors he wants to grant you, and for all those he has granted you up to the present."[2]

*Lord, don't ever let me rely on my own strength; help me to always rely on yours. Thank you for everything you've done — and will do — for me. Amen.*

# *Problems*

Ephesians 3:20-21: "Now to him who by the power at work within us is able to accomplish abundantly far more than all we can ask or imagine, to him be glory. . . ."[1]

*But when my problems bury me, I can't see God working within me.*

Padre Pio's assurance: "Be comforted because the hand of God that sustains you has not been taken away. Oh, yes, he is everybody's Father, but in a most singular way, he is such for the unhappy. . . . Dispel those sad clouds from your spirit, which the evil spirit continually increases in you in order to throw you into the arms of desperation — if that were possible. The heavenly Father wants to make you similar to his divine Son in the anguish of the desert and the ascent to Calvary. May this assurance be of sweet and exquisite comfort to you, in the midst of all those humiliations of which you have been made worthy, through no merit of yours."[2]

"God, the author of all grace and of every gift leading to salvation, has decreed that glory will be ours on condition that we endure suffering with a Christian spirit. So let us lift up our hearts, full of confidence in God alone. . . . God will always take more care of us than we can ask or imagine."[3]

*Lord, forgive me for complaining and losing faith. Help me to accept my problems and to trust that you will work them all out for the good. Amen.*

# *Spiritual Reading*

Matthew 7:7: ". . . search, and you will find. . . ."[1]

*But sometimes I don't know what I'm searching for or where to find it.*

Padre Pio's assurance: ". . . by reading sacred scripture and other holy and pious books we are seeking God."[2]

"I point out to you the power of holy reading to lead even worldly persons to change their course and enter on the path of perfection. . . . Who was it that won this great man [Saint Augustine] over to God? His ultimate conqueror was neither his mother, by her tears, nor the great Saint Ambrose, by his eloquence, but the reading of a [spiritual] book.

"But while Saint Augustine battled with tumultuous feelings, he heard a voice which [told him to read the scriptures]. As he read a chapter of Saint Paul, the thick darkness in his mind was dispelled. . . . From that moment, he made a clean break with the world, the devil, and the flesh, and devoted himself completely to the service of God. . . ."[3]

"Now, if the reading of holy books has the power to convert worldly men and women into spiritual persons, how very powerful must not such reading be in leading spiritual men and women to greater perfection?"[4]

*Lord, motivate me every day to read sacred scripture and other spiritual books, so that I discover your will for me — and the grace to follow it. Amen.*

# *Reflect, Consider*

Hebrews 12:1-2: ". . . let us run with perseverance the race that is set before us, looking to Jesus the pioneer and perfecter of our faith, who for the sake of the joy that was set before him endured the cross, disregarding its shame, and has taken his seat at the right hand of the throne of God."[1]

*But the "race" and the weight of the cross exhaust me.*

Padre Pio's assurance: "In order to imitate him [Jesus], we must reflect each day on the life of the one we intend to take as our model. From reflection is born esteem for his acts, and from esteem springs the desire and consolation of imitation."[2]

"You exclaim with him on the cross, 'My God, my God, why have you forsaken me?'[3] But reflect a while on the fact that the suffering humanity of the Lord was never truly abandoned by God. You are suffering all the effects of divine abandonment, but you have never been abandoned. And it is so also for those [other] souls who love Jesus. They suffer everything, even the trial of abandonment, but God is always with them. Therefore, be assured that Jesus is always with you and loves you because he is pleased with you. So, don't be afraid; let Jesus treat you as he wishes."[4]

*Lord, inspire me by your example, and enable me by your power and love, to never give up the "race," but to run with my eyes always on you. Amen.*

# Rejected, Abandoned by God

Deuteronomy 4:31: "Because the LORD your God is a merciful God, he will neither abandon you nor destroy you; he will not forget the covenant with your ancestors that he swore to them."[1]

*But why, in my sufferings, does it _feel_ as if he has abandoned me?*

Padre Pio's assurance: "Your present state is directly desired by God for your good. You must do nothing but resign yourself and bless the hand that seems to reject you. I say 'seems' because in reality the Father's hand never rejects, but it calls, embraces, and caresses, and if it sometimes beats you, it is always a paternal hand. In times of darkness and aridity, rest assured that, even if the sky seems to be made of bronze, it is still serene in your soul. It is true that you don't see this serenity in that state, but . . . believe that serenity is shining."[2]

"Trust in Jesus and do not be afraid, for you have no reason whatever to fear. Our most tender Savior has not forsaken you, but is showing his love for you. . . . The evil one wants to persuade you that you are the victim of his attacks and are abandoned by God. Don't believe him. Despise him in the name of Jesus and his most holy Mother."[3]

*Lord, when misery tries to make me believe you've abandoned me, help me to let go of fear and to trust that you hold me in your loving embrace. Amen.*

Padre Pio urged all to give up sin, take up their cross, follow Jesus, and find the joy God promised. "Serve God with a joyful spirit because God is the God of joy" (*Letters, Volume III*).

# Resigned to God's Will

Luke 22:42: "Father, if you are willing, remove this cup from me; yet not my will but yours be done."[1]

*But I'm not divine like Jesus; how can I have the strength and courage to ask God to let me suffer according to his will, rather than according to mine?*

Padre Pio's assurance: "When will my exile end? I am sorry about it, but I am resigned to God's will. May the divine plan be accomplished in me as long as it is for the glory of our dear Jesus. At certain times I suffer deeply in my soul, and if it were not for the occasional interruption of this torment, who knows what would become of me. Yes, this merciful Lord of ours hastens to my aid when the trial is at its height, and like the loving Father he is, he seems to console and encourage me. It is true that I suffer, but I do not complain because Jesus wishes things like this."[2]

"I struggle and sigh and weep; I cry out in complaint, but all in vain, until finally my poor soul, crushed by sorrow and with no more strength left, turns to the Lord and says, 'Not my will but yours be done.' "[3]

"My soul must endure a continual combat, but I see no other way out than to abandon myself into the arms of Jesus. . . ."[4]

*Lord, give me the courage to abandon myself to your will, confident that you will, when necessary, console and encourage me. Amen.*

# *Resist*

1 Peter 5:9: "Resist him [the devil], steadfast in your faith. . . ."[1]

*But how can I resist evil when it stalks and tempts me?*

Padre Pio's assurance: "Drive away [resist] what the enemy is whispering loudly in your ear when he wants you to believe you are almost on the point of being lost. Despise these evil insinuations and live in peace, for the Lord is with you as never before in your tribulations. . . . Take heart, then, and don't be afraid, for it is quite certain that the one who fears to be lost will not be lost, and that the one who fights with his eyes fixed on God will cry victory and intone the triumphal hymn. There is nothing to fear, for the heavenly Father has promised us the necessary help to prevent us from being overcome by temptations."[2]

"Always despise him [the enemy] and arm yourself against him with increasing steadfastness of faith, as it is written, 'Like a roaring lion your adversary the devil prowls around, looking for someone to devour. Resist him, steadfast in your faith.'[3] Don't let the many snares of this infernal beast frighten you. Jesus, who is always with you and who will fight with and for you, will never permit you to be tricked and overcome."[4]

*Lord, arm me with faith so that, even when the enemy roars and tries to lure me into his evil ways, I will listen to and obey only you. Amen.*

# Round About You

Psalm 34:7: "The angel of the LORD encamps / around those who fear him, and delivers them."[1]

*But if God would assign an angel just to watch over me, how would that angel help me?*

Padre Pio's assurance: "The companion of my childhood [my guardian angel] tries to lessen the pains which those impure apostates [enemies] inflict on me, by cradling my soul in a dream of hope."[2]

"Never say you are alone in sustaining the battle against your enemies. Never say you have nobody to whom you can open up and confide. You would do this heavenly messenger [your guardian angel] a grave wrong.

"Always keep him present to your mind's eye. Often remember the presence of this angel; thank him, pray to him, always keep him good company. Open up yourself to him and confide your suffering to him. Have a constant fear of offending the purity of his gaze. Know this and keep it well imprinted on your mind. He is so delicate, so sensitive. Turn to him in times of supreme anxiety, and you will experience his beneficial help."[3]

*Lord, though I find it hard to believe that you've assigned an angel just to help me, I accept this gift. Thank you for your infinite love which surrounds me, even through a guardian angel. Amen.*

# Sacred Heart of Jesus

Psalm 84:5: "Happy are those whose strength is in you, / in whose heart are the highways to Zion [heaven]."[1]

*But how can I go about finding my strength in God?*

Padre Pio's assurance: "Unite your heart with the heart of Jesus and be simple-hearted as he desires."[2]

"What happiness it would be if one day, returning from holy Mass, you were to find your miserable and poor heart outside your breast, and in its place you found the precious heart of our God. But, as we must not desire such great and extraordinary things, I at least desire that our hearts live only under obedience and by the commandments of the heart of this Lord.

"In this way we would be sweet, humble, and charitable because the heart of our divine Master has no law more lovable than that of sweetness, humility, and charity."[3]

"Don't ever fall back on yourself when the storm is raging. Place all your trust in the heart of our most sweet Jesus, who is not only mine but your Jesus also. Renew your faith continually and never give it up, for faith never abandons anyone, much less a soul that is yearning to love God."[4]

*Lord, I do yearn to love you more and more. Help me to place all my trust in your sacred heart, no matter what happens. Amen.*

# Sacred Scripture

2 Timothy 3:16-17: "All scripture is inspired by God and is useful for teaching, for reproof, for correction, and for training in righteousness, so that everyone who belongs to God may be proficient, equipped for every good work."[1]

*But I don't have time to study the Bible.*

Padre Pio's assurance: "This spiritual reading is as necessary to you as the air we breathe."[2]

"Always resolve to generously correspond to grace, rendering yourself worthy of him [Jesus], that is, similar to him in his adorable perfections, so well-known from the scripture and especially the Gospels. But in order to achieve this, we must reflect every day on his life. From reflection and meditation is born an esteem for his actions, and from esteem springs the desire to imitate him, along with the consolation gained from this."[3]

"Jesus is and will always be yours, and nobody will take him from you. Isn't this sufficient for you? Assiduously study Jesus Christ and his divine doctrine, and follow his illustrious example which he places before us as a model, in divine scripture, and do not fear the roaring tempest. . . ."[4]

*Lord, help me every day to take time to read sacred scripture, especially the Gospels, in order to learn about and follow you. Amen.*

# *Saints*

Revelation 7:9 ". . . there was a great multitude that no one could count, from every nation, from all tribes and peoples and languages, standing before the throne and before the Lamb. . . ."[1]

*But how can I — certainly no saint — ever hope to arrive at that throne?*

Padre Pio's assurance: "The knowledge of your interior unworthiness and sinfulness is an extremely pure divine light by which your very being and your ability to commit any sin, without the help of grace, is placed before your consideration.

"That light is due to the great mercy of God and was granted to the greatest saints, because it positions their souls in a place sheltered from all feelings of vanity or pride, thus consolidating humility which is the foundation of true virtue and Christian perfection."[2]

"Happy are we who, contrary to our every merit, are already on the hill of Calvary by divine mercy. We have already been made worthy to follow the heavenly Master; we have already been numbered among that blessed group of chosen souls, and all this through a most special act of divine mercy. . . . Let us not allow this blessed group to disappear from sight."[3]

*Lord, thank you for the knowledge that I do not deserve to forever praise you in heaven, but that, by your mercy, I will do so. Amen.*

**141**

# *Salvation*

Acts 4:12: "There is salvation in no one else [but Jesus]. . . ."[1]

*But if Jesus saves me today, what about all my tomorrows?*

Padre Pio's assurance: "Is it possible that the Lord will allow my downfall? Unhappily this is what I deserve, but can it be that the heavenly Father's goodness will be outdone by my wickedness? This will never, never be. I feel again the love of my God rising up like a giant in my poor heart, and I still have the confidence and strength to cry aloud with Saint Peter, 'Lord, save me!' "[2]

"No, God could not lose you, when, in order to avoid losing him, you persist in your resolutions. Let the world turn upside down, let everything be in darkness, in smoke, in confusion, but God is with us; what can we fear? If God lives in the darkness, and on Mount Sinai amid the thunder and lightning, shouldn't we be happy knowing we are close to him?"[3]

"May Jesus be always with you, may he sustain you in all the trials which he sends you out of sheer goodness, and may he fulfill in you his holy will for your salvation and for the salvation of all the other souls he wants to save."[4]

*Lord, thank you for forever saving me. Use me to save others. Amen.*

# Sanctify

1 Thessalonians 5:23: "May the God of peace himself sanctify you entirely. . . ."[1]

*But in the middle of trials, how can I be certain of my sanctification?*

Padre Pio's assurance: "When it [trial] comes from God, directly willed or indirectly permitted, we must be certain that all will work out always for the glory of Jesus and our greater sanctification."[2]

"Christian perfection obliges us to all this, and the Apostle exhorts us to act in this way, telling us with wisdom that 'you have clothed yourselves with the new self, which is being renewed in knowledge according to the image of its creator.'[3] But what is this new nature? It is our nature made holy by Baptism which, according to the principles of sanctification, must live in 'holiness and righteousness before him all our days.'[4]

"We Christians are images of God twice over, by nature and by grace. By nature we are given intelligence, memory, and will; by grace we are made holy through our Baptism, which imprints on our souls the beautiful image of God. Yes, sanctifying grace impresses the image of God upon us in such a way that we ourselves become divine by participation. . . ."[5]

*Lord, thank you for making me in your image; I ask for your saving grace. Amen.*

# *Scruples, Sadness, Fear*

Matthew 10:29-30: "Are not two sparrows sold for a penny? Yet not one of them will fall to the ground apart from your Father. And even the hairs of your head are all counted. So do not be afraid; you are of more value than many sparrows."[1]

*But sadness and anxiety still attack my soul when I sin or simply err.*

Padre Pio's assurance: "Beware of scruples. Spend a great deal of time in the presence of God. Beware of anxiety and restlessness because there is nothing that more greatly impedes progress towards perfection. Sweetly place your heart in the wounds of our Lord, but not with force. Have great confidence in his mercy because he will never abandon you. But do not fail, for this reason, to tightly embrace his holy cross."[2]

"When you are uncertain, or rather, in doubt as to whether or not you mortally offended God — may God preserve you from this — act as follows: Make an act of contrition and go forward. What else?"[3]

"Never permit your soul to become sad; to live with a sad scrupulous spirit, because Jesus is the spirit of sweetness, and is completely lovable toward those who want to love him."[4]

*Lord, rather than waste time in anxiety and self-condemnation, help me to always ask your forgiveness, get up, and go forward with you. Amen.*

# *Seasons of the Soul*

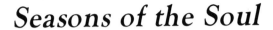

Song of Solomon 2:11-12: "For now the winter is past, / the rain is over and gone. / The flowers appear on the earth; / the time of singing has come. . . ."[1]

*But sometimes when spring arrives outside, winter still freezes my soul.*

Padre Pio's assurance: "Sometimes you feel the winter of so much sterility, distraction, listlessness, and boredom, and sometimes the dews of the month of May with the perfume of [good deeds and penance]. . . . Nothing remains but the autumn which does not bear too much fruit, but it often happens that, when the grain is threshed and the grapes crushed, you find the harvest is greater than it had promised.

"You would like it to be eternally spring and summer. But no, these rotations are necessary, both internally and externally. Only in heaven will everything be spring as regards beauty, autumn as regards enjoyment, and summer as regards love. There will be no winter, but here winter is necessary in order to practice abnegation and those beautiful virtues. . . ."[2]

"Do not fear the storm that roars around your heart, because to the degree the winter is rigid and stormy, on an equal basis will the spring be beautiful and rich with flowers, and the harvest more abundant."[3]

*Lord, remind me that, when winter storms surround my heart, they promise a more beautiful spring and abundant autumn. Amen.*

Concerning the Blessed Sacrament, Padre Pio wrote, "How could I, who am so weak and half-hearted, live without this Eucharistic food?" (*Letters, Volume II*).

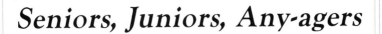

# *Seniors, Juniors, Any-agers*

Psalm 92:12, 14: "The righteous flourish like the palm tree. . . . In old age they still produce fruit; / they are always green and full of sap."[1]

*But others say I can't "produce fruit" if I'm "too young" or "too old."*

Padre Pio's assurance: "You must cultivate this [your] well-formed heart carefully and spare nothing which could be useful to its happiness. Even though in every season, that is at every age, you can and must do this, your present age is the most suitable."[2]

"It is a most singular grace to begin to serve this great God, when the flush of age renders us susceptible to all impressions. Oh, how this gift is acceptable when one offers the flowers with the first fruits of the tree."[3]

"And what can restrain you from making a total offering of your entire self to the good God, by deciding, once and for all, to give the world, the devil, and the flesh a kick, as our Godparents did for us in a determined manner when they held us at Baptism? Perhaps the Lord doesn't deserve this further sacrifice from you?"[4]

"May your heart and those of all souls belonging to Jesus always be possessed by and permeated with divine love!"[5]

*Lord, don't let me believe people when they tell me I'm "too young" or "too old" for you to use me for your good purposes. Amen.*

# Separated From God?

John 20:14: "... she turned around and saw Jesus standing there, but she did not know that it was Jesus."[1]

*But even though Jesus promises to stay beside me, sometimes I think he deserts me.*

Padre Pio's assurance: "One day Mary Magdalene was speaking to Christ, and believing herself to be separated from him, she cried and questioned him, and she was so anxious that, seeing him, she did not see him. What she saw, she thought, was the gardener. It is precisely the same thing that is taking place within you.

"So, courage, do not be anxious about anything. You have the divine Master in your company; you have not been separated from him. This is the truth and the only truth. What are you complaining about, then? Come on. ... You must have a strong heart. And as long as your soul has a strong will to live and die serving and loving God, do not be upset either by darkness or powerlessness, or any other impediment.

"Up there [in heaven], there will be no more obstacles; down here, we must still bear them. It is sufficient for us to know that God is our God, and that our heart is his home."[2]

*Lord, thank you that — even when it seems as if you have left me — you still dwell in my heart. Please make it a holy home for yourself. Amen.*

# *Servants of the Lord*

Isaiah 54:17: "No weapon that is fashioned against you shall prosper. . . . This is the heritage of the servants of the LORD. . . ."[1]

*But why then, when trouble assaults me, doesn't God console me instead of letting me wallow in misery?*

Padre Pio's assurance: "Live tranquilly for charity's sake, and don't fear divine work. Live totally in God, and for the love he holds for you, patiently bear all your miseries. Remember that in order to be a good servant of God, it is not necessary to be always consoled, always to be in a state of sweetness, always without contradiction.

"On the contrary, in order to be good servants of God, we must be charitable toward our neighbor, have an inviolable determination to do the will of God, have profound humility and simplicity in order to confide in God, picking ourselves up again many times when we fall, and tranquilly bearing others in their imperfections."[2]

"May it [grace of the Holy Spirit] give you strength to endure the fight and trial to which Jesus is subjecting you for your own sanctification and the edification of many others. May you . . . enjoy grace and peace from God."[3]

*Lord, forgive me my self-pity. Free me from it, so that I may serve you by serving others in love. Amen.*

# *Silence*

Ecclesiastes 3:1, 7: "For everything there is a season, and a time for every matter under heaven: . . . a time to keep silence, and a time to speak."[1]

*But sometimes I don't know what to say to God, and I remain silent.*

Padre Pio's assurance: "In the ways of the Lord, stop in your room, like the courtesans [servants], and pay him homage. He who will see this will be pleased with your patience, will favor your silence. . . ."[2]

"How many courtesans come and go a hundred times in the King's presence, not to speak or listen to him, but simply in order to be seen by him, and to let themselves be seen as his true servants? This manner of staying in the presence of God . . . is most holy and most excellent, most pure and extremely perfect. He will speak to you, will take a thousand walks in your company along the paths of the garden of prayer, and if this never happens, which would be impossible . . . be content just the same because it is our obligation to follow him. . . .

"Therefore, when you find yourself close to God in prayer, speak to him if you can, and if you are unable to do so, stay this way. Let yourself be seen, and do not disturb yourself further."[3]

*Lord, thank you for accepting my times of silent, as well as vocal, prayer. Thank you for the peace and joy of resting in your presence. Amen.*

# *Simplicity*

Matthew 18:3: "Truly I tell you, unless you change and become like children, you will never enter the kingdom of heaven."[1]

*But how can I become like a child?*

Padre Pio's assurance: "I recommend holy simplicity to you. Always look ahead without troubling too much in reflecting on the dangers you see at a distance. These seem to you to be an enormous army, but they are nothing; they are only pruned willow trees. Don't give it any importance, otherwise you could make a wrong move."[2]

"We must have great confidence in divine providence in order to practice holy simplicity."[3]

"Jesus likes to give himself to simple souls; we must make an effort to acquire this beautiful virtue of simplicity. . . . Jesus said, 'Unless you change and become like children, you will never enter the kingdom of heaven.'[4] But before he taught us this by his words, he had already put it into practice. He became a child and gave us the example of that simplicity he was to teach us later also by his words. . . . We must try to keep our thoughts pure, our ideas upright and honest, and our intentions holy."[5]

*Lord, cleanse my mind and heart; make me like a child: simple, honest, and always trusting in your tender love and guardianship. Thank you. Amen.*

# Sin

Romans 6:23: "For the wages of sin is death, but the free gift of God is eternal life in Christ Jesus our Lord."[1]

*But I thought I had to earn my way to heaven. I've made too many mistakes and committed too many sins for God to simply give me — without great sacrifices and painful penance on my part — his gift of salvation.*

Padre Pio's assurance: "Aren't your shortcomings and ingratitude of the past consumed by divine love?"[2]

"If you do good, praise and thank the Lord for it; if you happen to sin, humble yourself, propose to do better, ask for help, and keep on traveling the right path. I know very well that you do not want to sin; anything else must serve only to make you more humble."[3]

"Jesus did not measure his blood for the salvation of humankind, and is he likely to measure my sins to allow me to be lost? I do not think so. Soon and in a holy manner, he will redeem by his holy love this most ungrateful of his creatures."[4]

"Have no fear and do not afflict yourself anymore for the past because this has been pardoned by the Lord's goodness."[5]

*Lord, thank you for your unfathomable mercy and the free gift of eternal life which you bought for me with your most precious blood. Amen.*

# *Solitude*

Matthew 14:23: "And after he had dismissed the crowds, he went up the mountain by himself to pray."[1]

*But how can I get away to pray in solitude when my family, friends, others, and my duties demand my attention?*

Padre Pio's assurance: "Try to withdraw during the day, whenever possible, and in the silence of your heart, and in solitude, offer your praises, your blessings, your contrite and humble heart, and your entire self to the heavenly Father. Thus, while the goodness of the divine spouse is forgotten by the majority of his creatures made in his own image, let us remain always close to him by these periods of withdrawal and these exercises."[2]

"Lovingly humble yourself before God and people because God speaks to the humble. Love silence because much talk is never without sin. Withdraw into yourself as much as you can, because in this way the Lord speaks freely to the soul, and the soul is more able to listen to his voice."[3]

"The Lord has placed my soul in a state of greater detachment from the things of this base world, and I feel that he is strengthening more and more within me a holy freedom of spirit."[4]

*Lord, help me to withdraw into solitude whenever possible — and however brief — in order to offer myself to you and to listen to your voice. Amen.*

# *Soul*

Psalm 49:15: "But God will ransom my soul from the power of [hell]."[1]

*But a frigid darkness shrouds my soul. Why would God rescue me?*

Padre Pio's assurance: "Tell me, is it the sun or is it darkness that lights up and discloses things? God alone is his grace, God alone is the supreme Sun, and all others are nothing, or if they are anything, it is due to him alone. God alone can enlighten the soul with grace and show that soul what it is. And the more fully a person knows his own wretchedness and unworthiness in God's sight, the more remarkable is the grace that enlightens him and reveals to him what he is.

"I understand that the discovery of your own wretchedness under the action of this divine Sun saddens and distresses at the outset. It is a source of pain and of terror for the poor soul that is enlightened in this manner. But console yourself in our most sweet Lord, for when this divine Sun will have warmed the earth of your soul with its burning rays, it will cause new plants to spring up, which in due course will yield most delicious fruits.

"Believe me, for this is exactly how things stand. Console yourself, then, with this delightful thought, with this beautiful assurance."[2]

*Lord, when frigid darkness floods my soul, warm and brighten my soul with your eternal Sun, and make love, peace, and faith thrive within me. Amen.*

# *Spouse of Your Soul*

Psalm 63:1, 3: "O God, you are my God, I seek you, / my soul thirsts for you. . . . Because your steadfast love is better than life. . . ."[1]

*But how should I seek God, and how will I know that I've found him?*

Padre Pio's assurance: "Leave all concern to the most sweet spouse of souls. Lay your head on the breast of this most tender spouse as a beloved disciple and do not fear the uproar of the enemy, for the heavenly Master will not allow a hair of your head to be touched, just as he did not allow his disciples to be harmed in the garden of Gethsemane.

"Prostrate yourself before the Lord with humility of heart, like King Jehoshaphat when he was oppressed and grievously afflicted by the great multitude of enemies that surrounded him. And lift up your voice to the Lord in the same words of this holy King, 'We do not know what to do, but our eyes are on you.'[2] Because we do not know what to do, because we are deprived of every means and do not know how to ward off the evil, we can do no more than turn our eyes upon God, so that he may assist us in our needs in the manner most pleasing to God.

"Have no fear, for the Lord is with you."[3]

*Spouse of my soul, I place all my troubles and fears in your loving arms. Regardless of the uproar of my enemies, I will trust in you. Amen.*

# Stand Firm on the Word and Law of God

Ephesians 6:13, 17: "Therefore take up the whole armor of God, so that you may be able to withstand on that evil day, and having done everything, to stand firm. . . . Take the helmet of salvation, and the sword of the Spirit, which is the word of God."[1]

*But when temptation attacks, my soul trembles in help-lessness. How can I use the "sword of the Spirit," God's word, his law, to withstand evil?*

Padre Pio's assurance: "I must suggest the suitable means for the attainment of Christian perfection. The Apostle [Paul] suggests two most powerful means, which are the constant study of God's law [word] and the performance of all our actions for his glory.

"As regards the first means, he writes to the Colossians, 'Let the word of Christ dwell in you richly.'[2] . . . If the Christian is full of God's law which warns and teaches him to despise the world and its allurements, wealth and honors, and all that prevents him from loving God, he will never fail, no matter what adversities may befall him; he will endure everything steadfastly and perseveringly; he will readily forgive offenses and give thanks to God for all things."[3]

*Lord, help me to allow your word to always dwell in me, so that, by that "sword of your Spirit," I will stand firm against evil. Amen.*

In daily Mass, Padre Pio acted as a vessel through whom God reached out to others. "I think that the Holy Eucharist is a great means through which to aspire to perfection" (*Letters, Volume III*).

# *Storm*

Matthew 14:24, 27-29: "But by this time the boat, battered by the waves, was far from the land, for the wind was against them. . . . But immediately Jesus spoke to them and said, 'Take heart, it is I; do not be afraid.' Peter answered him, 'Lord, if it is you, command me to come to you on the water.' Jesus said, 'Come.' "[1]

*But when storms rage, I'd sink if I tried to walk on their "waters."*

Padre Pio's assurance: "The divine Master commanded Saint Peter to walk on the waters. And when Saint Peter heard the wind blowing and saw the dangerous storm, he was afraid, and this fear almost submerged him. So he asked the Master's help, and Jesus reprimanded him, saying, 'You of little faith, why did you doubt?'[2] And holding out his hand to him, the Master assured him. If God lets you walk on the stormy waters of adversity, do not doubt, do not be afraid. God is with you; have courage, and you will be delivered."[3]

"I still feel a holy joy by reason of God's great love for you. The storm that is raging around your soul is a sure sign of this love."[4]

"May Jesus be with you always!"[5]

*Lord, when storms batter against me, give me courage and faith to walk on the "water" with you and to not drown. Amen.*

# *Your Strength*

Isaiah 12:2: ". . . I will trust, and will not be afraid, for the Lord God is my strength and my might; he has become my salvation."[1]

*But if God strengthens me, why do I blunder so often?*

Padre Pio's assurance: "To be worried because something we have done has not turned out in accordance with our pure intention shows a lack of humility. This is a clear sign that the person concerned has not entrusted the success of his action to the divine assistance, but has depended too much on his own strength."[2]

"Do not let yourself be overcome by the fear of not loving God and consequently not saving yourself. . . . I know that no soul can worthily love its God. But when this soul does everything possible, and trusts in divine mercy, why should Jesus reject it? Doesn't he perhaps command us to love God in accordance with our strength, and not as he deserves? Therefore, if you have given and consecrated everything to God, why do you fear? . . . Tell our good God to do himself what you cannot do. Say to Jesus, 'Do you want more love from me? I have no more. Give me some more, and I'll offer it to you.' Do not doubt. Jesus will accept the offering. . . ."[3]

*Lord, forgive me for depending too much on my own strength. Help me to always place my trust in you and to allow you to become my strength. Amen.*

# Suffering

1 Peter 5:10: "And after you have suffered for a little while, the God of all grace . . . will himself restore, support, strengthen, and establish you."[1]

*But why does God allow suffering in the first place?*

Padre Pio's assurance: "All I can say is that my soul in this state [of suffering] seems to glimpse a concealed hand which can be none other than the hand of God. Moreover, at the apex of my spirit I feel, like the stirring of a gentle spring breeze, the divine Master's most beautiful assurance that not a hair of our heads will perish[2] without permission of our heavenly Father, that he watches over the soul with fatherly love. . . .

"Hence it is that the bitterness of the trial is sweetened by the balm of God's goodness and mercy. Praise be to God who can so marvelously alternate joy and tears so as to lead the soul by unknown paths to the attainment of perfection, a flower which the merciful God causes to bloom amid the thorns of suffering. . . ."[3]

"Don't be afraid, for no suffering will go unrewarded in eternal life. Trust and hope in the merits of Jesus, and in this way even poor clay will become finest gold which will shine in the palace of the King of heaven."[4]

*Lord, thank you for the assurance that, even in my suffering, your loving hand guides me and will never allow trials to defeat me. Amen.*

# *Supreme Good*

Matthew 19:17: "There is only one who is good."[1]

*I want to contain that supreme good in my heart, but I can't.*

Padre Pio's assurance: "Do not complain if you are still unable to definitively embrace the supreme good. The time will come when you will possess it definitively and totally."[2]

"The bitterness of love is still sweet and its weight suave. Therefore, why do you continually say, when feeling its great transports, that you are unable to contain it? Your heart is small, but it is expandable, and when it can no longer contain the grandeur of the beloved, and resist its immense pressure, do not fear, because he is both inside and out; by pouring himself into the interior, he will surround the walls. Like an open shell in the ocean, you will drink your fill, and exuberantly you will be surrounded and carried along by his power."[3]

"God's supreme goodness will therefore keep the nest of our hearts safe from the assaults of the world, with his holy love. . . ."[4]

"May God be pleased to continue with his divine work until you reach total possession of him, the supreme good."[5]

*Lord, fill and surround my poor, small heart, so that it will forever float in the ocean of your love, safe from the assaults of the world. Amen.*

# Sweetness

2 Corinthians 2:15: "For we are the aroma [sweet savor] of Christ to God among those who are being saved and among those who are perishing."[1]

*But I certainly don't feel sweet. How do I obtain this sweetness?*

Padre Pio's assurance: "I recommend that you practice holy sweetness in a particular way, in all misfortunes which often present themselves in this life. Be tranquil and at peace, always keeping our Lord in your heart. How happy you will be if you are steadfast in the hands of the divine majesty amidst your worries and as you go about your daily tasks, which will be extremely pleasant because God will help you. And the slightest consolation you feel will be greater than any the world could give.

"In order to obtain this interior and exterior sweetness, before doing anything else every day, you should pray that the Lord might grant you true sweetness of spirit. . . . Make the resolution to practice this virtue, particularly towards those people to whom you have a greater duty.

"You should undertake this task of mastering yourself, calling it to mind a hundred times a day. . . . You will be happy if you do this because God will dwell in your heart and will reign there tranquilly."[2]

*Lord, daily teach me how to practice holy sweetness, so that I will always please you and bring joy to those around me. Amen.*

# *Temple of God*

2 Corinthians 6:16: "For we are the temple of the living God; as God said, 'I will live in them and walk among them, and I will be their God, and they shall be my people.' "[1]

*If God dwells in me, why doesn't he prevent my sufferings?*

Padre Pio's assurance: "Up there [in heaven], there will no longer be any obstacles [to our reaching perfection], but down here we must put up with them. Suffice it to know that God is our God, and let our hearts be his temple."[2]

"Among other pious considerations, remember that our soul is the temple of God, and as such, we must keep it pure and spotless before God and his angels. Let us blush for having given access to the devil and his snares many times — with his enticements to the world, his pomp, his calling to the flesh — by not being able to keep our hearts pure and our bodies chaste; for having allowed our enemies to insinuate themselves into our hearts, thus desecrating the temple of God which we became through holy Baptism."[3]

"In the hour of trial, don't tire yourself in trying to find God. He is within you, even then, in a most intimate manner."[4]

*Lord, thank you that, even in my troubles, you dwell inside me, loving me and making sure that I don't suffer more than I can bear. Amen.*

# Temptation's Tests

1 Corinthians 10:13: "No testing [temptation] has over-taken you that is not common to everyone. God is faithful, and he will not let you be tested beyond your strength, but with the testing he will also provide the way out so that you may be able to endure it."[1]

*But when temptation strikes, my trust in God vanishes.*

Padre Pio's assurance: "Don't let temptations alarm you. They are the trials of the soul that God wants to test, seeing it strong enough. . . ."[2]

"Temptations are the merchandise offered by the enemy, but do not fear him, rather despise him. As long as he makes an uproar, it is a sign that he has not yet possessed the will. . . . Let your will always be contrary to his suggestions and live tranquilly because you are not at fault. . . ."[3]

"Don't make an effort to overcome your temptations because these efforts would strengthen them. Despise them and do not dwell on them. Call to your imagination Jesus Christ crucified in your arms and on your breast. And say, kissing his side a number of times, 'This is my hope, the living source of my happiness. I will hold you tightly, Jesus, and will not let you go until you have placed me in a safe place.' "[4]

*Lord, I have dwelt on my temptations, thinking that was the only way to overcome them. Help me, instead, to always let go of them and trust you. Amen.*

# *Thanks and Praise*

1 Thessalonians 5:18: "Give thanks in all circumstances. . . ."[1]

Hebrews 13:15: "Through him [Jesus], let us continually offer a sacrifice of praise to God. . . ."[2]

*But I don't have time during the hectic day to thank and praise God.*

Padre Pio's assurance: "Protected, covered, and defended by the uniform of this dear Lord, let us stand before him and pray with the humility of the creature and the confidence and freedom of a child. And given that God loves to delight in us, let nothing in the world distract us from delighting in him and contemplating his grandeur and infinite titles, by which he has a right to our praises and love. Let us pray to him that he be generous as usual with his divine help, so that, through us, his holy name may be greatly praised and blessed, so that we, too, can say in truth, with our heavenly Mother, 'My soul magnifies the Lord.' "[3]

"Will my entire life be long enough to thank the heavenly Father for his goodness, for the continual and most singular favors he grants to one who offends him continually? Blessed forever be our good God who does not know how to punish this wretched soul. . . ."[4]

*Lord, often remind me to lift up my heart to you in silent thanks and praise, even amid the commotion of each twenty-four-hour period. Amen.*

# *This Kindhearted Angel*

Matthew 26:53: "Do you think that I cannot appeal to my Father, and he will at once send me more than twelve legions of angels?"[1]

*But I'm not Jesus; why would God send me even one angel?*

Padre Pio's assurance: "What have I ever done to deserve such exquisite kindliness on the part of my [guardian] angel? But I do not worry about this, by any means. Isn't the Lord free to bestow his graces on whomsoever he wills and in the way that pleases him?"[2]

"You should frequently invoke your guardian angel, this kindhearted angel. Often repeat the beautiful prayer, 'Angel of God, my guardian — to whom the goodness of the heavenly Father entrusts me — enlighten, protect, and guide me, now and forever.' What a consolation will be yours when, at the hour of death, you will behold this good angel who accompanied you during life and was so generous in his motherly care of you. Oh, may this delightful thought make you increasingly fond of Jesus' cross, as this is also the wish of your good angel.

"Oh, he [your angel] is so considerate and so sensitive. . . . How dear he is and how good."[3]

*Lord, thank you for the guardian angel you have assigned to me. Help me to always acknowledge, trust, thank, and love this kindhearted angel. Amen.*

# *Tomorrow*

Matthew 6:34: "So do not worry about tomorrow, for tomorrow will bring worries of its own. Today's trouble is enough for today."[1]

*But don't I need to worry about tomorrow, so I'll be prepared?*

Padre Pio's assurance: "Always have a firm and general proposition to serve God with all your heart and for the whole of your life. Don't worry about tomorrow; think only of doing good today, and when tomorrow comes, it will be today, and then it is time enough to think of it."[2]

"We must imitate the people of God when they were in the desert. These people were severely forbidden to gather more manna than they needed for one day.[3] Do not doubt that God will provide for the next day, and all the days of our pilgrimage."[4]

"Do you know what the shepherds do when they hear thunder and see the air filled with lightning? They retire with their flocks under the laurel bushes. Now let us do the same. When we see that persecutions and contradictions give us a forewarning of some great displeasure, we must retire with great confidence under the cross, along with our affections, because all will work out to the benefit of those who try to love God."[5]

*Lord, I place all my tomorrows into your loving hands. Help me to always seek you first and to trust that you will provide for me. Amen.*

Padre Pio urged all to receive Holy Communion. "Never fail to eat the food of the angels" (*Letters, Volume I*).

# *Tranquillity, Stillness, Peace*

Mark 4:39-40: "He woke up and rebuked the wind, and said to the sea, 'Peace! Be still!' Then the wind ceased, and there was a dead calm. He said to them, 'Why are you afraid? Have you still no faith?' "[1]

*But when the storms of life buffet me, how can I rid myself of fear?*

Padre Pio's assurance: "Before anything else, we should try to live in tranquillity of spirit. Not because tranquillity is the mother of Christian content, but because it is the daughter of the love of God and of the resignation of our own will. We can have occasion to practice this daily because contradictions are never lacking. . . ."[2]

"You must endeavor to place your soul, agitated through the work of the evil spirit, in this state of rest and tranquillity — reminding yourself of the spiritual rest which our hearts must always have — in the will of God, wherever it takes us. Live as God pleases in this valley of miseries, with total submission to his holy will. How much indebted to divine goodness we are; this divine goodness which has made us ardently desire to live and die in his divine love. Let us hope that this great Savior, who gives us the will to live and die in his love, may give us the grace to do so."[3]

*Lord, give me the grace to live and die in your love, submitted to your will. And help me to always find my spiritual tranquillity in you. Amen.*

# Troubles, Trials, and Tribulations

John 14:1: "Do not let your hearts be troubled."[1]

*But troubles wait for me everywhere, ready to attack.*

Padre Pio's assurance: "Call to mind the words the divine Master said to the Apostles, and which he says to you today, 'Do not let your hearts be troubled.'[2] Yes, do not let your heart be troubled in the hour of trial because Jesus has promised his real assistance to those who follow him."[3]

"Tribulation is more precious than gold and rest, to those whom God has chosen. 'I would rather be a doorkeeper in the house of my God than live in the tents of wickedness.'[4] Now during these days, you have been in a state of extreme discouragement in the house of our Lord, but the agony that tortured your heart did not cause you to lose hope in divine goodness. On the contrary, you always conformed your will to that of God's, and with your will, you assiduously dwelled on the holy mount of Calvary. So the Lord wishes to reward the sadness you bore for love of him."[5]

"In the midst of the trials which may afflict you, just place all your confidence in our supreme good, in the knowledge that he takes more care of us than a mother takes of her child."[6]

*Lord, thank you for being an ever-present father and mother to me, always loving, always caring. Help me to conform my will to yours. Amen.*

# *Trust in God*

Isaiah 30:15: ". . . In quietness and in trust shall be your strength."[1]

*But how do I know — if I trust in God — that he won't let me fall? Everyone else I've ever trusted has let me down.*

Padre Pio's assurance: "Fortify yourself with prayer, humility, and unlimited trust in divine help. Abandon yourself as a beloved child of the heavenly Father in his most loving arms, and do not fear the war waged against you by Satan. He is powerless against the soul that places all its trust in God alone. He [Satan] will wage war, in so far as he is permitted to do so from above, and God will never permit you to be tempted beyond your strength."[2]

"Once again, then, I urge you to have ever-greater confidence in God, for it is written that those who trust in him will never be forsaken."[3]

"But be quite sure that it is Jesus who loves you. Abandon yourself to his holy actions, and do not fear because Jesus is with you and is pleased with you.[4] Arm yourself with the beautiful trust in the Lord, and take heed of the assurances which God gives you through me."[5]

*Lord, help me to ignore the enemy when he pounds on the door of my heart. Keep me always trusting in you and believing your promises. Amen.*

# *Unseen*

2 Corinthians 4:17-18: "For this slight momentary affliction is preparing us for an eternal weight of glory beyond all measure, because we look not at what can be seen but at what cannot be seen; for what can be seen is temporary, but what cannot be seen is eternal."[1]

*But how can I look at something that I cannot see?*

Padre Pio's assurance: "Let us withdraw our gaze from those things which are visible to our eyes — by which I mean worldly goods — the sight of which fascinates and distracts the soul and contaminates the heart. Worldly goods prevent us from keeping our eyes fixed on our heavenly home."[2]

"What should we say if we were to behold a poor peasant almost stupefied as he continued to gaze at a swiftly flowing river? Perhaps we should just begin to laugh at him, and with good reason. Is it not folly to fix our gaze on something that is rapidly passing? This, then, is the state of a person who fixes his eyes on visible things."[3]

"Let the consideration of all those good things to be possessed in that realm [heaven] provide us with delightful food for our thoughts."[4]

*Lord, rather than focus on the things of this world that I can see, help me to fix my sight on you and your heavenly kingdom which I cannot see. Amen.*

# *Virtue, Piety*

Matthew 6:1: "Beware of practicing your piety before others in order to be seen by them; for then you have no reward from your Father in heaven."[1]

*But why not?*

Padre Pio's assurance: "You should conceal the good your beloved is operating in you. The virtues are to be kept as a person keeps a treasure, which, if not hidden from the sight of envious people, will be seized. The devil is always on the watch; he is the most envious of all, and he seeks to seize at once this treasure consisting of the virtues as soon as he recognizes it. This he does by having us attacked by the powerful enemy which is vain glory.

"In order to preserve us from this great adversary, our Lord, who is always concerned for our good, warns us on this point in various parts of the Gospel. Does he not tell us that when we want to pray we should go into our room, shut the door so as not to be seen by anyone, and pray to our Father who is in secret?[2] . . . That when we give alms we should not let our right hand know what our left hand is doing?"[3]

"Invariably direct your actions to the pure glory of God."[4]

*Lord, forgive me for all the times I've flaunted my holy deeds and possessions. Thanks for all the good you give to me and do through me. Amen.*

# Deep Waters

Psalm 69:2, 15: "I have come into deep waters, / and the flood sweeps over me. . . . Do not let the flood sweep over me. . . ."¹

*But why does God allow a flood of troubles in the first place?*

Padre Pio's assurance: "Take heart because the Lord is with you; he suffers with you, groans with you, and is pleased with you. . . . Don't you yearn to love him forever? Therefore, have no fear.

"Even if you were to have committed all the sins of this world, Jesus tells you, 'Your sins, which were many, have been forgiven; hence you have shown great love.'² But then you will say to me, what is the reason for this trial of abandonment of my poor soul? It is the trial of heavenly love. 'I have come into deep waters, and the flood sweeps over me.'³

"This is the trial of souls who are particularly loved by that Jesus who was pleased to experience all the fear of that moral tempest in the desert, the garden, and Calvary. Every soul that wants to be saved must undergo something of that mysterious storm because every predestined soul must resemble Jesus. Well then, haven't you chosen Jesus as your portion? Therefore, let him treat you as he pleases."⁴

*Lord, though I don't want trials, I accept them, knowing that you'll use them to make me more like you. Help me to love and serve you forever. Amen.*

# Weaknesses

2 Corinthians 12:8-9: "Three times I appealed to the Lord about this [trial], that it would leave me, but he said to me, 'My grace is sufficient for you, for power is made perfect in weakness.' "[1]

*But I worry that God will abandon me because of my weaknesses.*

Padre Pio's assurance: "Heavenly goodness permits weaknesses, not in order to abandon you, but to render you humble and more steadfast, more firm and more tightly attached to the hand of this divine mercy."[2]

"Do not lose heart, but in your weakness, unite yourself more to Jesus who speaks to you through wise advisers. When the words of comfort and the voice of your wise director calm you after your anxiety, this is a sign that you are dear to Jesus."[3]

"Take comfort in our most sweet Lord, as you should know that the soul's greatest misery is when it doesn't feel weak, but feels strong; when it trusts in itself; when it is overconfident.

"Oh, if only all souls could experience such a holy weakness, we would not see so many souls fall at every instant. A soul who felt its weakness and had recourse to God for help has never fallen."[4]

*Lord, I feel my weakness every moment of every day. Help me to always place my confidence in you, for in my weakness you are strong. Amen.*

# When God Hides

Mark 15:34: ". . . My God, my God, why have you forsaken me?"[1]

*But, surrounded by the darkness of my troubles, I cry out to God, and I ask, as Jesus did on the cross, "Why have you forsaken me?"*

Padre Pio's assurance: "You are right to complain at finding yourself more often than not in darkness. You seek your God, you sigh for him, you call him and cannot always find him. Then it seems to you that God hides himself, that he has abandoned you. But, I repeat, do not fear. Jesus is with you, and you are with him. In darkness, times of tribulation, and spiritual anxiety, Jesus is with you. In that state, you see nothing but darkness in your spirit, but I assure you, on behalf of God, that the light of the Lord invades and surrounds your entire spirit. You see yourself in tribulations, and God repeats to you through the mouth of his prophet and that of authority, 'I will be with them in trouble.'[2] You see yourself in a state of abandonment, but I assure you that Jesus holds you more tightly than ever to his divine heart. Even our Lord on the cross complained of the Father's abandonment.[3] But did the Father ever — and could he ever — abandon his Son?"[4]

*Lord, thank you that — even when I can see only darkness — your light of love and protection shines outward from where you dwell within my spirit. Amen.*

# *Bloom Where You're Planted*

Psalm 1:3: "They are like trees planted by streams of water, / which yield their fruit in its season, / and their leaves do not wither."[1]

*But, where God has planted me, I find boredom, toil, weariness, and pain. How can God use me here? How can I ever bear "fruit"?*

Padre Pio's assurance: "Take courage and begin the work of your salvation on the path where God places you. What do you expect? We must see and speak to God amid the thunder and turmoil. We must see him in the bush, amid the fire and thorns, and in order to achieve all this we should go barefoot, totally renouncing our own will and affections. Submit yourself entirely to the will of God and keep far from you the suggestion — which is certainly not God's but the enemy's — that you would serve God better in a different state. God is served only when he is served according to his will."[2]

"He wants to speak to us in the midst of the thorns, the bush, the cloud, and the lightning, like he did to Moses,[3] and we want him to speak to us in a sweet and fresh aura, as he did to Elijah.[4] But what are you afraid of? Listen to our Lord who says to Abram and to you also, 'Do not be afraid, Abram, I am your shield.' "[5]

*Lord, help me to renounce my will and to submit entirely to yours. Speak to me, and I will listen, for I love you, my Lord and my God. Amen.*

# Will of God

Matthew 6:9-10: "Pray then in this way: Our Father in heaven, hallowed be your name. Your kingdom come. Your will be done. . . ."[1]

*But sometimes I don't want to submit to God's will, especially when it promises hardship, tedium, and pain.*

Padre Pio's assurance: "Let us adore God's will and be ready to conform our will in all things and at all times to the will of God. In this way we shall give glory to the heavenly Father, and everything will be to our advantage for eternal life.

"God, who has bestowed so many benefits on us, is satisfied with such an insignificant gift as that of our will. Let us offer it to him along with the divine Master himself in that most sublime prayer, 'Our Father in heaven, hallowed be your name. Your kingdom come. Your will be done, on earth as it is in heaven.'[2] . . . Let us hand it [our will] over to God in a total offering, and let us do this also in our daily life."[3]

"May the grace of the Holy Spirit make you more worthy of the heavenly kingdom. May Jesus and Mary comfort you, sustain you, and bless you all the time. Amen."[4]

*Lord, enable me to always know, love, and obey your will. Comfort, sustain, and bless me, as I seek to follow you. Amen.*

# Bibliography

Di Flumeri, Fr. Gerardo, O.F.M. Cap. *Homage To Padre Pio*. San Giovanni Rotondo, Italy: Our Lady of Grace Capuchin Friary, 1982.

Di Flumeri, Fr. Gerardo, O.F.M. Cap., editor. *Padre Pio of Pietrelcina Letters, Volumes I and II*. San Giovanni Rotondo, Italy, 1994.

Gaudiose, Dorothy M. *Prophet of the People*. New York: Alba House, 1974.

McGregor, Fr. Augustine, O.C.S.O. *Padre Pio: His Early Years*. San Giovanni Rotondo, Italy: Our Lady of Grace Capuchin Friary, 1981.

*The New Revised Standard Version Bible: Catholic Edition*. Tennessee: Catholic Bible Press, 1993.

Parente, Fr. Alessio, O.F.M. Cap., editor. *Padre Pio of Pietrelcina Letters, Volume III*. San Giovanni Rotondo, Italy, 1994.

Parente, Fr. Alessio, O.F.M. Cap. *Send Me your Guardian Angel*. San Giovanni Rotondo, Italy: Our Lady of Grace Capuchin Friary, 1984.

Ruffin, C. Bernard. *Padre Pio: The True Story (Revised and Expanded)*. Indiana: Our Sunday Visitor, Inc., 1991.

Schug, Fr. John A., Cap. *Padre Pio: He Bore the Stigmata*. Indiana: Our Sunday Visitor, Inc., 1976.

# *Notes*

(Except for some minor editing in order to clarify, condense, and create a more inclusive text, all of Padre Pio's quotes — taken from *Padre Pio of Pietrelcina's Letters*, Volumes I, II, and III — are reproduced practically verbatim. The *Letters* were obtained from the National Centre for Padre Pio, 2213 Old Route 100, Barto, PA 19504.)

Introduction
1. *Padre Pio of Pietrelcina's Letters*,
   *Volume III*, p. 895
2. *Ibid.,* p. 492
3. *Ibid.,* p. 310
4. *Ibid.,* pp. 102-103
5. *Ibid.,* pp. 728-729
6. John 14:1
7. *Volume III*, p. 263
8. *Volume III*, p. 491

Meditation 1
1. Matthew 16:24-25
2. *Letters, Volume I*, p. 427
3. *Letters, Volume III*, p. 258
4. *Ibid.,* p. 1032

Meditation 2
1. Hebrews 6:18-19
2. *Volume III*, p. 111
3. *Ibid.,* p. 112
4. *Ibid.,* pp. 111-112

Meditation 3
1. Matthew 6:25, 32, 34
2. *Volume III*, p. 730

Meditation 4
1. Ephesians 6:14-17
2. John 14:1
3. *Volume III*, p. 841

Meditation 5
1. Romans 12:4-6
2. *Volume III*, pp. 288-289

Meditation 6
1. Luke 6:18-19
2. *Volume III*, p. 714
3. Matthew 6:10
4. *Volume II*, p. 358
5. *Volume III*, p. 507

Meditation 7
1. John 3:29
2. *Volume III*, p. 307
3. *Volume II*, pp. 111-112

Meditation 8
1. Matthew 11:28-30
2. *Ibid.,* 11:30
3. *Volume II*, p. 385
4. *Volume III*, p. 543
5. *Volume I*, p. 1086

Meditation 9
1. Psalm 107:28-29
2. *Volume I*, p. 666
3. *Ibid.,* pp. 678-679
4. *Ibid.,* p. 679

Meditation 10
1. 1 Peter 5:7
2. *Volume III*, pp. 995-996
3. *Ibid.,* p. 131

4. *Volume II*, p. 152
5. *Ibid.,* p. 153

Meditation 11
1. Colossians 3:14
2. *Volume II*, pp. 399-400

Meditation 12
1. Proverbs 15:13
2. *Volume II*, p. 76
3. *Ibid.,* p. 84
4. *Volume III*, p. 779
5. *Ibid.,* pp. 69-70
6. *Volume I*, p. 243

Meditation 13
1. Luke 18:16-17
2. *Volume III*, pp. 730-731
3. *Ibid.,* p. 940
4. *Ibid.,* p. 736

Meditation 14
1. Colossians 3:16
2. *Volume II*, p. 250

Meditation 15
1. Matthew 2:10-11
2. *Volume III*, pp. 888-889

Meditation 16
1. Isaiah 61:1-2
2. Acts 9:31
3. *Volume III*, p. 464
4. *Ibid.,* p. 438

Meditation 17
1. Mark 2:16-17
2. *Volume III*, p. 305
3. *Ibid.*

Meditation 18
1. John 3:17-18
2. *Volume III*, p. 781
3. *Ibid.,* p. 782

Meditation 19
1. Proverbs 3:26

2. Hebrews 3:6
3. *Volume I*, p. 519
4. *Volume II*, p. 320
5. *Ibid.*

Meditation 20
1. 2 Corinthians 1:5
2. *Volume I*, p. 318
3. *Ibid.,* p. 227
4. *Ibid.,* p. 299
5. *Ibid.,* p. 224

Meditation 21
1. Luke 10:42
2. Romans 8:26
3. *Volume II*, pp. 312-313
4. *Ibid.,* p. 315
5. *Volume III*, pp. 568-569

Meditation 22
1. Psalm 27:14
2. Psalm 91:15
3. *Volume II*, p. 320
4. *Volume III*, p. 302
5. *Ibid.,* p. 401

Meditation 23
1. Mark 8:34
2. *Volume I*, pp. 923-924
3. *Ibid.,* p. 382
4. *Ibid.,* p. 519
5. *Ibid.,* p. 1086

Meditation 24
1. Romans 8:35, 37
2. *Volume III*, p. 687
3. *Ibid.,* pp. 563-564
4. *Volume II*, p. 187

Meditation 25
1. Psalm 116:15
2. Romans 6:5
3. Isaiah 25:7
4. *Volume III*, p. 729

Meditation 26
1. Psalm 19:12

2. *Volume III*, p. 584
3. *Ibid.,* pp. 510-511
4. *Ibid.,* p. 583
5. *Ibid.,* pp. 506-507

Meditation 27
1. Proverbs 8:30-31
2. *Volume III*, pp. 100-101

Meditation 28
1. 1 Peter 2:2
2. Hebrews 11:16
3. *Volume III*, p. 686
4. *Ibid.,* p. 687
5. *Ibid.,* p. 582

Meditation 29
1. Luke 1:78-79
2. *Volume III*, p. 547
3. *Ibid.,* p. 549
4. *Ibid.,* p. 550

Meditation 30
1. Hebrews 5:7
2. *Volume II*, pp. 504-505

Meditation 31
1. 1 Thessalonians 5:17
2. *Volume III*, p. 714
3. *Ibid.,* p. 715

Meditation 32
1. Romans 9:21
2. *Volume III*, p. 663
3. Luke 21:19
4. *Volume III*, pp. 664-665

Meditation 33
1. Psalm 61:8
2. *Volume III*, pp. 841-842
3. *Ibid.,* p. 108
4. *Volume III*, p. 108

Meditation 34
1. Isaiah 35:6-7
2. *Volume III*, pp. 521-522
3. *Volume III*, p. 486

Meditation 35
1. 1 Thessalonians 5:14
2. *Volume III*, pp. 996-997
3. *Ibid.,* p. 107

Meditation 36
1. Luke 1:72-74
2. *Volume I*, pp. 244-245
3. *Volume III*, p. 788

Meditation 37
1. John 17:24
2. *Ibid.*
3. *Volume II*, pp. 211-212

Meditation 38
1. Matthew 6:11
2. *Ibid.*
3. *Volume II*, pp. 357-358

Meditation 39
1. Romans 7:21-24
2. *Volume III*, p. 511
3. *Ibid.*
4. Romans 7:24-25

Meditation 40
1. 1 Peter 5:8
2. *Ibid.,* 5:9
3. *Volume II*, p. 262

Meditation 41
1. Mark 4:37-39
2. Matthew 14:30-31
3. *Volume III*, p. 936

Meditation 42
1. Luke 21:18
2. *Ibid.*
3. *Volume III*, p. 832
4. *Ibid.,* p. 833

Meditation 43
1. Psalm 23:4
2. *Volume I*, p. 456
3. *Volume III*, p. 276

Meditation 44
1. Matthew 26:26
2. *Volume I*, p. 426
3. *Volume III*, pp. 451-452
4. *Ibid.*, p. 452
5. Matthew 6:11
6. *Volume II*, p. 359

Meditation 45
1. Psalm 17:5
2. *Volume III*, pp. 540-541
3. *Ibid.*, p. 540

Meditation 46
1. Colossians 3:13-14
2. *Volume II*, p. 248
3. *Ibid.*, p. 249

Meditation 47
1. John 8:31-32
2. Matthew 6:10
3. *Volume III*, p. 57

Meditation 48
1. Isaiah 41:8-10
2. John 8:12
3. Matthew 2:2
4. Psalm 36:9
5. *Volume III*, pp. 404-405

Meditation 49
1. 1 Corinthians 15:51-53
2. *Volume III*, p. 833
3. *Ibid.*, p. 713

Meditation 50
1. 1 Corinthians 4-7
2. James 1:17
3. *Ibid.*
4. Matthew 19:17
5. *Volume I*, p. 448

Meditation 51
1. Romans 8:13
2. *Volume III*, p. 305
3. *Ibid.*, p. 258
4. *Volume II*, p. 274

Meditation 52
1. 1 Peter 2:9
2. *Volume I*, p. 690
3. *Ibid.*, p. 730

Meditation 53
1. Psalm 91:11
2. *Volume II*, p. 292
3. *Ibid.*, p. 420
4. *Ibid.*, p. 389

Meditation 54
1. Isaiah 58:11
2. *Volume III*, pp. 541-542

Meditation 55
1. Luke 1:38
2. *Volume III*, pp. 51-52
3. *Volume I*, pp. 672-673

Meditation 56
1. Psalm 144:15
2. *Volume I*, p. 308
3. *Volume III*, p. 506

Meditation 57
1. 3 John 2
2. *Volume III*, p. 330
3. *Volume II*, p. 241
4. *Ibid.*, p. 242

Meditation 58
1. Matthew 11:29
2. *Volume III*, pp. 971-972
3. *Ibid.*, p. 971

Meditation 59
1. Proverbs 23:26
2. *Ibid.*
3. Matthew 25:1-13
4. *Volume II*, p. 489

Meditation 60
1. 1 Peter 1:3-4
2. *Volume III*, p. 706
3. *Ibid.*, p. 452
4. *Volume I*, p. 427

5. *Volume III*, p. 553
6. *Ibid.,* p. 933

Meditation 61
1. Hebrews 4:16
2. *Volume III*, p. 261
3. *Ibid.,* p. 262
4. *Ibid.,* p. 461
5. *Ibid.,* p. 261

Meditation 62
1. Matthew 5:48
2. *Volume III*, p. 288
3. *Ibid.,* p. 89
4. *Volume II*, p. 564

Meditation 63
1. Romans 8:27
2. Hebrews 7:25
3. John 1:29
4. *Volume II*, p. 69
5. *Ibid.,* p. 70
6. *Ibid.,* p. 110

Meditation 64
1. Matthew 28:19
2. 1 Corinthians 3:17
3. Philippians 2:6
4. Colossians 2:9-10
5. *Volume II*, p. 236
6. *Ibid.,* p. 237
7. *Ibid.,* p. 435

Meditation 65
1. 1 Peter 1:21
2. *Volume II*, p. 410
3. *Volume III*, p. 418
4. *Volume I*, p. 739

Meditation 66
1. 1 Peter 5:5
2. *Volume I*, p. 1269
3. *Volume III*, pp. 116-117
4. 1 Peter 5:6
5. *Ibid.*
6. *Volume III*, p. 167

Meditation 67
1. John 7:37-39
2. *Ibid.,* 7:37-38
3. *Volume I*, p. 744
4. *Ibid.,* p. 745

Meditation 68
1. Hebrews 6:15
2. *Volume III*, pp. 60-61
3. *Ibid.,* p. 102

Meditation 69
1. James 1:34
2. *Volume III*, p. 435
3. *Ibid.,* p. 583
4. *Ibid.,* p. 684
5. *Ibid.,* p. 686
6. *Ibid.,* p. 684

Meditation 70
1. Isaiah 66:13
2. *Volume II*, p. 69
3. *Volume III*, p. 736
4. *Ibid.,* p. 286
5. *Ibid.,* p. 285

Meditation 71
1. 1 John 2:15-17
2. *Volume III*, pp. 860-861

Meditation 72
1. Luke 2:7
2. *Volume III*, p. 569
3. *Ibid.,* p. 704

Meditation 73
1. 1 Thessalonians 4:1
2. *Volume III*, p. 998

Meditation 74
1. 1 Timothy 2:1
2. *Volume III*, p. 767
3. *Ibid.,* pp. 769-770
4. *Ibid.,* p. 99

Meditation 75
1. James 5:11
2. Psalm 103:13-14
3. *Volume I*, p. 346
4. *Ibid.*, p. 347

Meditation 76
1. 1 Peter 4:12-13
2. *Volume I*, p. 342
3. *Ibid.*, p. 343

Meditation 77
1. John 16:22
2. *Ibid.*
3. *Volume II*, p. 214

Meditation 78
1. Romans 5:1-2
2. Romans 4:24-25
3. *Volume II*, p. 212
4. *Ibid.*, pp. 212-213

Meditation 79
1. Song of Solomon 1:2
2. *Ibid.*, 1:1-2
3. *Volume I*, pp. 455-456
4. *Ibid.*, p. 456

Meditation 80
1. Luke 11:9
2. *Ibid.*
3. *Volume II*, p. 470

Meditation 81
1. Psalm 91:12
2. *Volume III*, pp. 84-85
3. *Volume II*, p. 478

Meditation 82
1. Galatians 2:19-20
2. *Volume III*, p. 338
3. *Volume I*, p. 431
4. *Ibid.*, p. 370
5. *Volume II*, p. 510

Meditation 83
1. Luke 16:10

2. *Volume III*, pp. 707-708
3. *Ibid.*, p. 676

Meditation 84
1. Psalm 33:20-22
2. *Volume I*, p. 357
3. *Volume II*, p. 279
4. *Ibid.*, pp. 506-507
5. *Ibid.*, p. 509

Meditation 85
1. Matthew 22:37
2. *Volume II*, p. 423
3. *Ibid.*, p. 425
4. *Ibid.*, p. 424

Meditation 86
1. Luke 10:27
2. *Volume II*, p. 215
3. *Ibid.*, p. 216
4. *Volume III*, p. 1073

Meditation 87
1. Luke 7:47-48, 50
2. *Volume II*, p. 505
3. *Ibid.*, p. 506

Meditation 88
1. Revelation 12:5
2. *Volume I*, p. 311
3. *Ibid.*, p. 254

Meditation 89
1. Romans 8:28
2. *Volume III*, p. 830
3. *Ibid.*, pp. 831-832

Meditation 90
1. Psalm 19:14
2. *Volume III*, p. 255
3. *Ibid.*, p. 256
4. *Ibid.*, p. 73

Meditation 91
1. 1 Timothy 1:15-16
2. *Volume III*, p. 757
3. *Ibid.*, p. 758

Meditation 92
1. Job 11:13, 16
2. Judges 16:17
3. *Volume III*, p. 179

Meditation 93
1. Matthew 18:10
2. *Volume II*, p. 421

Meditation 94
1. Luke 1:48-49
2. *Volume I*, p. 673
3. *Ibid.*, p. 206
4. *Volume II*, p. 389
5. *Volume III*, p. 553

Meditation 95
1. Luke 23:42-43
2. *Volume I*, p. 237
3. *Ibid.*, p. 347
4. Matthew 19:26

Meditation 96
1. Isaiah 55:7
2. *Volume III*, pp. 270-271
3. *Volume II*, pp. 320-321

Meditation 97
1. Philippians 3:10, 21
2. *Volume III*, p. 69

Meditation 98
1. Psalm 23:3
2. Matthew 5:3
3. *Volume III*, pp. 269-270

Meditation 99
1. Luke 8:15
2. *Volume II*, p. 215
3. Luke 21:19
4. *Volume I*, pp. 992-993

Meditation 100
1. John 14:27
2. *Volume I*, p. 674

3. Matthew 11:30
4. *Volume I*, p. 678
5. *Volume III*, p. 769

Meditation 101
1. Hebrews 6:1
2. *Volume II*, p. 290
3. *Ibid.*, p. 216

Meditation 102
1. Colossians 3:17
2. Philippians 2:9
3. Acts 4:12
4. Philippians 2:10
5. *Volume II*, p. 237
6. *Volume II*, p. 250

Meditation 103
1. James 5:16
2. *Volume II*, p. 504
3. Genesis 28:12
4. *Volume II*, p. 505

Meditation 104
1. Ephesians 2:1, 8
2. *Volume II*, pp. 231-232

Meditation 105
1. Psalm 16:11
2. *Volume III*, p. 928
3. *Volume II*, p. 290
4. *Ibid.*, p. 291
5. *Volume III*, p. 991
6. *Volume II*, pp. 122-123

Meditation 106
1. Philippians 4:13
2. *Volume III*, pp. 72-73

Meditation 107
1. Ephesians 3:20-21
2. *Volume III*, pp. 130-131
3. *Volume II*, pp. 262-263

Meditation 108
1. Matthew 7:7
2. *Volume II*, p. 155

3. *Ibid.,* pp. 156-157
4. *Ibid.,* p. 158

Meditation 109
1. Hebrews 12:1-2
2. *Volume I*, p. 1116
3. Matthew 27:46
4. *Volume III*, p. 338

Meditation 110
1. Deuteronomy 4:31
2. *Volume III*, pp. 926-927
3. *Volume II*, pp. 69-70

Meditation 111
1. Luke 22:42
2. *Volume I*, p. 219
3. *Volume I*, p. 806
4. *Ibid.,* p. 544

Meditation 112
1. 1 Peter 5:9
2. *Volume II*, p. 411
3. 1 Peter 5:8-9
4. *Volume III*, p. 51

Meditation 113
1. Psalm 34:7
2. *Volume I*, p. 362
3. *Volume III*, p. 85

Meditation 114
1. Psalm 84:5
2. *Volume II*, p. 139
3. *Volume III*, pp. 608-609
4. *Volume II*, p. 377

Meditation 115
1. 2 Timothy 3:16-17
2. *Volume II*, p. 449
3. *Volume III*, p. 716
4. *Ibid.,* p. 791

Meditation 116
1. Revelation 7:9-10
2. *Volume III*, p. 548
3. *Ibid.,* p. 540

Meditation 117
1. Acts 4:12
2. *Volume I*, p. 618
3. *Volume III*, p. 584
4. *Volume II*, p. 557

Meditation 118
1. 1 Thessalonians 5:23-24
2. *Volume III*, p. 451
3. Colossians 3:10
4. Luke 1:75
5. *Volume II*, pp. 247-248

Meditation 119
1. Matthew 10:29-31
2. *Volume III*, pp. 710-711
3. *Ibid.,* p. 647
4. *Ibid.,* p. 779

Meditation 120
1. Song of Solomon 2:11-12
2. *Volume III*, p. 321
3. *Ibid.,* p. 736

Meditation 121
1. Psalm 92:12, 14
2. *Volume III*, pp. 421-422
3. *Ibid.,* p. 931
4. *Ibid.,* p. 422
5. *Ibid.,* p. 930

Meditation 122
1. John 20:14
2. *Volume III*, pp. 985-986

Meditation 123
1. Isaiah 54:17
2. *Volume III*, p. 932
3. *Volume II*, p. 319

Meditation 124
1. Ecclesiastes 3:1, 7
2. *Volume III*, p. 991
3. *Ibid.,* pp. 991-992

Meditation 125
1. Matthew 18:3
2. *Volume III*, p. 687
3. *Ibid.*, p. 688
4. Matthew 18:3
5. *Volume I*, pp. 677-678

Meditation 126
1. Romans 6:23
2. *Volume III*, p. 218
3. *Ibid.*, p. 757
4. *Volume I*, p. 237
5. *Volume III*, p. 996

Meditation 127
1. Matthew 14:23
2. *Volume II*, p. 189
3. *Volume III,*, p. 436
4. *Volume I*, p. 519

Meditation 128
1. Psalm 49:15
2. *Volume II*, p. 387

Meditation 129
1. Psalm 63:1, 3
2. 1 Kings 22
3. *Volume I*, pp. 486-487

Meditation 130
1. Ephesians 6:13, 17
2. Colossians 3:16
3. *Volume II*, pp. 249-250

Meditation 131
1. Matthew 14:24, 27-29
2. *Ibid.*, 14:31
3. *Volume III*, p. 833
4. *Volume I*, p. 1131
5. *Ibid.*, p. 1117

Meditation 132
1. Isaiah 12:2
2. *Volume II*, p. 290
3. *Volume III*, p. 726

Meditation 133
1. 1 Peter 5:10
2. Luke 21:18
3. *Volume I*, pp. 665-666
4. *Volume II*, p. 490

Meditation 134
1. Matthew 19:17
2. *Volume III*, p. 1041
3. *Ibid.*, p. 1040
4. *Ibid.*, p. 693
5. *Ibid.*, p. 357

Meditation 135
1. 2 Corinthians 2:15
2. *Volume III*, pp. 312-313

Meditation 136
1. 2 Corinthians 6:16
2. *Volume III*, pp. 754-755
3. *Ibid.*, p. 89
4. *Ibid.*, p. 338

Meditation 137
1. 1 Corinthians 10:13
2. *Volume III*, p. 354
3. *Ibid.*, p. 426
4. *Ibid.*, pp. 573-574

Meditation 138
1. 1 Thessalonians 5:18
2. Hebrews 13:15
3. *Volume III*, p. 101
4. *Volume I*, p. 601

Meditation 139
1. Matthew 26:53
2. *Volume I*, pp. 372-373
3. *Volume II*, pp. 421-422

Meditation 140
1. Matthew 6:34
2. *Volume III*, pp. 687-688
3. Exodus 16:13-21
4. *Volume III*, p. 688
5. *Ibid.*, p. 609

Meditation 141
1. Mark 4:39-40
2. *Volume III*, p. 928
3. *Ibid.*, pp. 110-111

Meditation 142
1. John 14:1
2. *Ibid.*
3. *Volume III*, pp. 491-492
4. Psalm 84:10
5. *Volume III*, pp. 917-918
6. *Volume II*, p. 260

Meditation 143
1. Isaiah 30:15
2. *Volume III*, p. 72
3. *Volume II*, p. 260
4. *Volume III*, p. 224
5 *Volume II*, p. 320

Meditation 144
1. 2 Corinthians 4:17-18
2. *Volume II*, p. 202
3. *Ibid.*, pp. 202-203
4. *Ibid.*, p. 203

Meditation 145
1. Matthew 6:1
2. *Ibid.*, 6:5-6
3. *Ibid.*, 6:2-3
4. *Volume I*, p. 449

Meditation 146
1. Psalm 69:2, 15
2. Luke 7:47
3. Psalm 69:2
4. *Volume III*, pp. 218-219

Meditation 147
1. 2 Corinthians 12:8-9
2. *Volume III*, p. 521
3. *Ibid.*, p. 532
4. *Ibid.*, p. 72

Meditation 148
1. Mark 15:34
2. Psalm 91:15
3. Mark 15:34
4. *Volume III*, p. 1038

Meditation 149
1. Psalm 1:3
2. *Volume III*, p. 542
3. Exodus
4. 1 Kings 19:12-13
5. *Volume III*, p. 583

Meditation 150
1. Matthew 6:9-10
2. *Ibid.*
3. *Volume II*, pp. 356-357
4. *Ibid.*, p. 355

Our Sunday Visitor...
# *Your Source for Discovering the Riches of the Catholic Faith*

Our Sunday Visitor has an extensive line of materials for young children, teens, and adults. Our books, Bibles, booklets, CD-ROMs, audios, and videos are available in bookstores worldwide.

To receive a FREE full-line catalog or for more information, call **Our Sunday Visitor** at **1-800-348-2440**. Or write, **Our Sunday Visitor** / 200 Noll Plaza / Huntington, IN 46750.

------------------------------------------------------------

**Our Sunday Visitor**
200 Noll Plaza
Huntington, IN 46750
**1-800-348-2440**
osvbooks@osv.com

*Your Source for Discovering the Riches of the Catholic Faith*